Following Christ

Across the Threshold

The Non-Initiate's Guide to Entering the Spiritual World

RON MACFARLANE

Published 2019 by
Greater Mysteries Publications
Mission, BC, Canada

Cover Design: Ron MacFarlane

Printed in the United States of America

ISBN:
ISBN-13: 978-0995967410
ISBN-10: 0995967415

DEDICATION

With profound reverence and eternal gratitude,
this work is dedicated to the saviour of mankind, Christ-Jesus,
who has re-established safe passage back to the spiritual world
for all who are willing to undertake the hazardous journey.
By faithfully following his wise direction
and the path that he himself forged after death,
even non-initiates (in accordance with their karmic-destiny)
may be afforded the tremendous opportunity
to consciously enter the spiritual world
and then safely return to
physical life
on earth.

CONTENTS

of Darkness

FOLLOWING CHRIST

ACROSS THE THRESHOLD

INTRODUCTION

THROUGHOUT THE MODERN age there has been a strong, commonly-held misconception (among religious and non-religious persons alike) that if there truly exists a spiritual world beyond the physical, it is impossible to know anything for certain until after death. And unfortunately (it is believed), no one has come back from death to verify spiritual existence or not. Surprisingly and happily, however, this popular belief turns out to be entirely untrue.

According to esoteric science, mankind has always had the capacity to not only contact the spiritual world *before* death; but on certain rare occasions, the soul is able to exit the physical body *prior to* death, briefly sojourn in the spiritual world and then safely return to the physical body afterwards.

In ancient times, it was only male "initiates"—that is, a small number of specially-selected and carefully-prepared adherents of one of the highly-secretive Mystery Centres in Europe, Asia, the Middle East and North Africa—who were afforded the special opportunity of consciously experiencing the spiritual world while still remaining alive on earth.

Unfortunately, consciously entering the spiritual world in the Mystery Centres involved a hazardous out-of-body procedure made possible by hypnotically placing the initiate into a death-like, comatose condition for three full days. If the initiate was successfully revived, all experience and information obtained while sojourning in the spiritual world (termed "gnosis") was secretly kept and closely guarded within the confines of the Mystery Centre—under the strictest penalty of death.

Fortunately, all this changed with the earthly incarnation of the god-man, Christ-Jesus. Through the transformative power of his own life, death, resurrection and ascension Christ-Jesus forged an entirely new path of secure entry into the spiritual world; as well as a new path of safe return to life on earth. This new Christian path replaced and superseded the dangerous initiatory practices and methods of the ancient Mystery Centres.

Hereafter, those seeking suitable entry into the spiritual world during life (and not simply waiting until death) had two legitimate initiatory paths made available by Christ-Jesus: (1) the path of Mystic-Christianity, and (2) the path of Rosicrucian-Christianity. Both initiatory paths were established though St. John the evangelist (not the apostle).[1]

The path of Mystic-Christianity focuses primarily on affective-emotional spirit-development, using the Gospel of John as the meditative guidebook. Moreover, this initiatory path has been specifically formulated for the stream of *exoteric* Christianity (the Church of St. Peter);[2] and has been commonly practiced within the various monastic orders for hundreds of years.

The path of Rosicrucian-Christianity focuses primarily on cognitive-intellectual spirit-development, using the techniques established during medieval times by the authentic Rosicrucian Order of adepts.[3] This initiatory path has been specifically formulated for the stream of *esoteric* Christianity, and for hundreds of years was secretly practiced exclusively within the hidden confines of Rosicrucian schools. Beginning in the early 1900s, however, a great deal of information regarding the Rosicrucian path of initiation was publicly revealed for the first time by eminent esotericist and initiate, Rudolf Steiner (1861–1925).[4]

What many esotericists are unaware of at the present time is that there exists a third avenue of conscious entry into the spiritual world made available by Christ-Jesus—specifically offered to non-initiates. This unique path has been made possible because of two profound superphysical developments: (1) since his world-altering ascension into the heavenly realm, Christ-Jesus has become the new "lord of karma" governing human evolutionary destiny; and (2) for the past two thousand years Christ-Jesus has been slowly raising the vibratory level within mankind's collective subconsciousness.

As a result, a relatively small number of present-day individuals—with no current initiatory training—have spontaneously experienced brief moments of supersensible perception. To some, Christ-Jesus has fleetingly appeared in his etheric, angel-like resurrection form; while to others he has been perceived as an internal, all-wise spirit-voice. And on even rarer occasions, Christ-Jesus—acting as spirit-guide (or "hierophant")—has consciously escorted non-initiates into the spiritual world for a brief sojourn while still alive, and then safely returned them to physical life on earth.

In all these instances of unexpected and unplanned spiritual encounters, there is a strong karmic (destiny)[5] component involved. Though the individuals involved may not have knowingly undertaken initiatory training in their present lifetimes, in most cases their inner souls were sufficiently prepared in previous lifetimes to enable these extraordinary experiences to occur. Moreover, Christ-Jesus—as the new lord of karma—has the power and authority to grant special dispensation to non-initiates whom he considers worthy of receiving extraordinary spiritual development.

This publication—*Following Christ Across the Threshold: The Non-Initiate's Guide to Entering the Spiritual World*—is not, therefore, a manual of initiatory training. But rather, it is intended as a step-by-step preparatory guide (in the form of a sequential series of "lessons") for non-initiates; in order to assist them as to "what to expect, how to react and what to do" if they are ever granted the opportunity—while still being physically alive—of entering the spiritual world under the inner direction of Christ-Jesus. Hopefully, this intellectual preparation will help alleviate some of the horrific, terrifying and soul-shattering experiences associated with consciously crossing the threshold into the spiritual world during life (and also after death).

Also worth noting for the sincere spiritual seeker, this guide is not a fabricated or theoretical discourse; but is based on profound first-hand experience, since this author—as a non-initiate in his twenty-first year of life—successfully followed Christ-Jesus across the threshold into the spiritual world, and then voluntarily assented to return to physical life in order to share this experience with others. "Thus you will know them by their fruits" (Matt 7:20).

LESSON 1:

NECESSARY KARMIC REQUIREMENTS

1.1 The Inherent Virtue of Moral Goodness

HAVING INCARNATED divine love within the collective soul of mankind for the very first time in world history, the salvational concern of Christ-Jesus universally extends to all human beings; regardless of age, religion, sex, race, nationality, social position, wealth or education. Furthermore, due to the illustrious example and world-transformative power of his life, death, resurrection and ascension, not only did Christ-Jesus assume the mantle of "world-saviour," but he also became the new "lord of karma" for all human development.

Consequently, in order to receive his supernal assistance and help, it's not necessary to belong to a particular Christian denomination, or even to be religiously inclined at all. His benevolent support even extends to those who have doubts concerning the very existence of God and the entire spiritual world. Instead, one of the necessary requirements for Christ-Jesus to grant special karmic dispensation for non-initiates to consciously cross the threshold is that they must inherently embody moral goodness as a characteristic virtue established over the course of numerous lifetimes. It matters little to the Lord of Karma if one believes in God or is atheistic; if one is educated or is unschooled; if one is Christian or is Hindu. What is important to safely enter the spiritual world under his special direction is that the non-initiate must intrinsically be a "good person," that he or she genuinely and habitually strives to do "the right thing" in life.

This of course is not to say that the Saviour of mankind has no interest in the malefactor or the wrongdoer. As the human embodiment of divine love, Christ-Jesus' compassionate salvational concern is directed to saint and sinner alike. However, those individuals with an inherently evil disposition will themselves deliberately reject good spiritual advice; and will therefore find it impossible to faithfully follow Christ-Jesus into the spiritual world.

In other words, even though Christ-Jesus as world-saviour compassionately and continually knocks on the inner door of every human soul, quietly calling out, "Follow me, for I AM the way"; it is unlikely that an immoral, dissolute or iniquitous soul will suddenly choose to faithfully follow Christ-Jesus across the threshold into the spiritual world, even if given the extraordinary opportunity.

1.2   The Sincere Desire for Truth

A second, karmically-acquired innate characteristic that a non-initiate must possess before any attempt to rightfully cross the threshold is a strong, deep-seated desire for truth. Without this inner propensity, it is unlikely that the non-initiate will be able to correctly discern the inner voice of Christ-Jesus that is critically necessary to consciously enter the spiritual world in the right way.

In Christ-Jesus, truth is not something that is external and merely conveyed or taught; but instead, truth is spiritual reality that is internalized and personally embodied. As such, Christ-Jesus does not biblically declare: "I have come to speak the truth"; but rather, "I AM the truth of which I speak" (to paraphrase Jn 14:6). Therefore, in today's Christian era the sincere desire and search for truth is synonymously the desire and search for Christ-Jesus.

Lacking a strong, internal sense of the Christ-truth, the non-initiate can easily enter the spiritual world in a corrupted way; and thereby acquire a distorted and falsified view of that world. Such is the case with black magicians who strive "to take heaven by force" (Matt 11:12).

1.3 Overcoming the Dark Spectre of Fear, Hatred and Doubt

Christian initiates are well aware that there is a powerfully-instinctive, subconscious hostility toward the existence of the spiritual world that must be overcome if one is to successfully cross the threshold in full awareness. This deep-seated animus is more than just fear, hated and doubt of the unknown—it actually arises intrapsychically from the accumulated evil that each soul has amassed over numerous lifetimes, and which is collectively retained in the subconscious mind.

This "shadow self," this "dark side" to our personality lies deeply hidden to ordinary awareness, and only becomes visible through supersensible perception. The covert existence of this malevolent karmic-accretion acts as a powerful barrier to entering the spiritual world. Consequently, those following the path of Rosicrucian-Christian initiation are specially trained to recognize, to understand and to overcome this karmic obstacle—referred to as the "lesser guardian of the threshold."

When perceived supersensibly for the first time—by initiates and non-initiates alike—this obstructive karmic-detritus will assume a horrifying spectral configuration. For the highly-trained initiate with developed superphysical senses, the spectral configuration is perceived as a composite of three beastly figures that are corruptions of thinking, feeling and willing.[6]

Since the non-initiate typically lacks developed supersensible perception, their spectral vision will predictably be less detailed, vivid and defined than that of a trained initiate. Moreover, the horrible apparitional-form that appears to the non-initiate will predictably be more individualized and culturally influenced than that of the initiate.[7]

For the non-initiate with undeveloped supersensible perception, unexpectedly encountering this loathsome apparition is predictably a much more terrifying and confusing experience than it is for the prepared initiate. For one thing, this spectral apparition usually happens by surprise; the non-initiate is completely unprepared for its appearance. For another thing, it appears as an external psychic projection; and as such, the untrained non-initiate is likely to regard it as an actual evil being who intends to do them harm.

When confronted with this frightening apparition, it is vitally important for initiate and non-initiate alike to courageously confront it, and not shrink back in fear. Or to phrase it differently, when objectively faced with the image of our own dark side, it is psychologically imperative that we face the awful truth that each of us—as a repeatedly re-embodied soul—has amassed a great deal of negative karma from our evil misdeeds in the past.

Having faced this disturbing truth, it is equally important not to despairingly conclude that we are hopelessly evil persons as a result. But instead, this spectral shadow-self is simply burdensome karmic baggage accumulated from numerous past lives. And though we subconsciously carry this baggage with us from lifetime to lifetime, it does not define who we are as basically-good and honest individuals.

Moreover, by facing the disturbing truth of a hidden dark-side, we are also presented with the positive opportunity to consciously counteract and diminish its disruptive existence by repeatedly performing good deeds instead.

Furthermore, by having our shadow-self raised up from the subconscious depths of our psyche into the bright light of day-awareness, there is less danger that the non-initiate will unknowingly ferry it across the threshold into the spiritual world. Such an occurrence would prove disastrous, since every perception and experience in the spiritual world would be distorted, falsified and eclipsed by this unwelcomed karmic-shadow of psychic darkness.

From the aforementioned, it should be apparent that—in one significant way—our karmic shadow-self performs a positive service for our overall spiritual development. By subconsciously blocking our access to the spiritual world until we consciously face and overcome its presence, our dark-side does indeed initially act as a benevolent "guardian of the threshold." Therefore, the non-initiate should not expect to be guided across the threshold by Christ-Jesus without having first successfully encountered and overcome this guardian. Only the foolhardy, the wicked and the various practitioners of the black arts will attempt to force their way past this powerful guardian.

Given the necessity of successfully overcoming their dark side, is there a way for the non-initiate to determine when and where such a supersensible, spectral encounter will occur? Unfortunately, given the right karmic conditions this frightening spectral encounter with their own incarnational evil can happen at any time, and anywhere. One could be alone on a dark night, or even in a crowded sunlit room when suddenly one is faced with the terrifying presence of psychic iniquity. It is intended that after reading this discourse, the non-initiate will recognize the experience and know what to do if and when it should occur.

LESSON 2:

THE CRUCIFIXION EXPERIENCE

2.1 Surrendering One's Entire Life to God

CHRIST-JESUS, BY HIS public crucifixion on the stage of world history (and not within the secret confines of a Mystery Centre) openly demonstrated for all time the new Christian method of safely crossing the threshold into the spiritual world. This of course is not to suggest in any way that one must also be physically nailed to a wooden cross until death in order to correctly follow his example. But rather, that in order to consciously "cross over" into the spiritual world, one must—through an intrapsychic act of child-like faith—be willing to place one's entire life-existence into the hands of God. Or as Christ-Jesus demonstrated before he himself crossed the threshold: "Father, into thy hands I commit my spirit!" (Lk 23:46).

This complete surrender to God is not as easy as perhaps one might think. One must be prepared to sever and disconnect all mental, emotional and physical attachments to life on earth, including: friends, family, possessions, accomplishments, memories, pleasures, plans, goals, aspirations, careers, thoughts, dreams, talents, abilities, body, mind and life itself. In other words, one freely chooses to completely surrender one's entire "self-existence" into God's care.

The esoteric key to understanding the historic crucifixion event—termed the "Mystery of Golgotha" in Rosicrucian teaching—is that it is not about Christ-Jesus sacrificing his physical life to atone for mankind's sins (as commonly believed). But instead, it is a public demonstration by Christ-Jesus on how to psychologically "die" to one's earthly-self and to the world; thereby consciously crossing over into the spiritual world and realizing one's true, spiritual God-self as a result.

The self-sacrificial act of freely surrendering one's entire life to God does not, therefore, require the destruction of the physical body. Rather, it is an internal, psychological act of the will that can be effectively undertaken even during life.

2.2 When is the Crucifixion Experience Likely to Occur for the Non-Initiate?

Apart from those with an esoteric background, many people in today's materialistic and secularized world are completely unaware that ordinary sleep involves the temporary and partial detachment of the soul from the body. In more esoteric terminology, the astral body and ego rise up out of the physical and etheric bodies during sleep (please refer to Figure 1 on the following page).[8] This bodily separation accounts for the observable fact that an individual in deep sleep exists in a vegetative state without self-awareness, conscious thought or emotion.

In other words, every time we go to sleep we actually cross the threshold into the spiritual world; but in an entirely unconscious way. This is primarily due to two main reasons.

Firstly, most people today have not developed the soul senses that are necessary for clear perception in the spiritual world.

DEGREES OF CONSCIOUSNESS	SANSKRIT TERMS	EGO (SELF)	VEHICLES OF EXPRESSION	INDIVIDUAL LEVELS OF EXISTENCE	COSMIC REALMS OF EXISTENCE
DIVINE CONSCIOUSNESS	ATMAN	THE HIGHER EGO (SELF)	SPIRIT-BODY	SPIRIT	CELESTIAL WORLD [SPIRIT LAND]
COSMIC CONSCIOUSNESS	BUDDHI	THE HIGHER EGO (SELF)	LIFE-SPIRIT	SPIRIT	
SPIRITUAL CONSCIOUSNESS	MANAS	THE HIGHER EGO (SELF)	SPIRIT-SELF	SPIRIT	
SOUL CONSCIOUSNESS	KAMA-RUPA	THE LOWER EGO (SELF)	CONSCIOUSNESS SOUL	SOUL	SOUL WORLD
SELF CONSCIOUSNESS	KAMA-RUPA	THE LOWER EGO (SELF)	INTELLECTUAL SOUL	SOUL	
WAKING CONSCIOUSNESS		THE LOWER EGO (SELF)	SENTIENT SOUL	SOUL	
DREAM CONSCIOUSNESS	LINGA-SHARIRA		ASTRAL BODY	BODY	PHYSICAL WORLD
SLEEP CONSCIOUSNESS	PRANA-JIVA		ETHERIC BODY	BODY	
TRANCE CONSCIOUSNESS	STHULA-SHARIRA		PHYSICAL BODY	BODY	

Figure 1: The Various Vehicles of Expression

Secondly, the dark guardian of fear, hatred and doubt that blocks access to the spiritual world automatically plunges the soul into a state of unconsciousness prior to crossing the threshold. This acts as a psychic veil of protection for the unprepared soul or the non-initiate.

The opportunity for a non-initiate to consciously cross the threshold, therefore, is most likely to occur during the natural process of falling asleep. Moreover, since an out-of-body journey with Christ-Jesus across the threshold—that mirrors his own death and resurrection—will usually take several hours to complete, it is highly unlikely to occur during regular daytime activity (such as working on the job, driving a car, taking a shower, walking on a street, conversing on a phone or eating at a restaurant).

Though less likely to occur for the non-initiate, consciously crossing the threshold can also take place during deep meditation, during which the astral body and ego exit the physical and etheric bodies. Without a definite separation of body and soul, the meditator is merely mentally "gazing across" the threshold into the spiritual world; and not actually "bodily crossing" the threshold and sojourning within the spiritual world.

2.3 Consciously Exiting the Physical Body during Sleep

Interestingly, as one has the familiar sensation of gradually "falling" asleep, of "descending" in conscious awareness, what is supersensibly occurring is the opposite—the astral body and ego are actually "rising up" out of the physical and etheric bodies. Since the etheric body retains the memory images of daily events, dreaming typically occurs as the two higher vehicles slowly disengage from the etheric (or memory) body. During this process, the various bodies and vehicles are temporarily misaligned which causes the dream imagery to be recognizably erratic, confused and eccentric.

Once the higher vehicles have fully withdrawn from the lower bodies (except for a silvery thread of contact—which acts as a superphysical "umbilical cord" in order to maintain physical life), then dreaming ceases, and the soul descends further into the unconsciousness of deep sleep. Upon returning to waking consciousness—out of the veiled unconsciousness of deep sleep—the ego and astral body reintegrate with the etheric and physical bodies. Once again, due to a temporary stage of misalignment with the etheric memory-body, a short period of disjointed dreaming typically occurs prior to waking up.

For the non-initiate, the first indication that they have been karmically granted the special opportunity of consciously crossing the threshold into the spiritual world is that as they are falling asleep, they don't begin to slip into dream-consciousness; but instead, continue to remain fully aware of themself. Nevertheless, during this preliminary stage of sleep the higher vehicles are beginning to slowly disengage from the lower bodies. As a result, the non-initiate will consciously experience the eerie sensation of actually rising upwards and leaving their physical body.

What typically occurs at this stage is the fearful thought— "Oh my God, I must be dying!" If one succumbs to this fear, then the higher vehicles quickly snap back into the lower bodies, and one instantly wakes up. However, if one continues to remain calm, recalling that this fearful emotion protectively issues from the dark guardian of the threshold, then one will continue to sense oneself rising up out of the body.

Non-initiates take note—this is the starting point of the crucifixion experience! Prior to the complete separation of the higher vehicles from the lower bodies, when dreaming normally occurs, the non-initiate must put their *complete* trust and confidence in God. If there is any doubt about doing so, then one has once again succumbed to the dark guardian of the threshold, and will quickly fall back into the unconsciousness of sleep or struggle to wake back up. As well, if there is anything that one is unable to surrender, and which attaches them to the physical world, then again, one will immediately fall into deep sleep or quickly reawaken.

If one has never consciously exited the physical body and crossed the threshold into the spiritual world before, then it is unarguably an overwhelming leap into vastly-unknown and potentially-dangerous territory. In this case, therefore, without knowing such things as: "What to expect? What will happen? What to do? Will one be harmed? or even, Will one survive?"—it makes reasonable sense to put one's complete trust in God—even if one is unsure of his existence.

For the non-initiate, the crucifixion experience may be induced and actuated by a severe existential crisis in life. It may be psychologically critical to find satisfactory answers to such profound questions as: "Is there a God? And if so, is it a benevolent deity or a malevolent one? What exactly is love? What is life? What is my own purpose in life?" Under such circumstances, it may not be a difficult struggle to offer up one's entire life to God. If it seems possible that there is *no* benevolent supreme-deity in existence, then life may not seem worth living anyway.

Nevertheless, even with a psychological willingness to give up everything in life to find answers to critically-debilitating questions, there is often one particular aspect of every non-initiate's self-existence that proves to be fearfully difficult to voluntarily surrender at this crucial moment, and that is one's thinking activity. Without being consciously aware of it, there is often a strange, deep-seated, subconscious notion that if thinking activity ever stopped, then one's selfhood would suddenly cease to exist. This notion that self-existence is entirely dependent on thinking has been succinctly expressed in Descartes' famous dictum—"I think, therefore I am."[9]

2.4 Stilling the Mind—A Foretaste of Nirvana

At the moment of the non-initiate's crucifixion experience, it may seem that the fear of stilling all mental activity is their own personal anxiety; but in fact, this trepidation constitutes a crucially-necessary step for everyone in order to completely self-surrender to the benevolence of God. By completely stilling the mind, the non-initiate silences their own self-generated inner voice; and is thereby, better able to discern the "still small voice" of the divine spirit within.

Instead of the fearfully-anticipated effect of self-annihilation, the complete cessation of all mental activity will engender the immersive experience of melting into a cosmic ocean of profound tranquility. For a brief, glorious moment in time it will feel as though the entire universe becomes absolutely still, with one's entire consciousness blissfully free from all earthly desires and attachments.[10]

Though the non-initiate may not realize it at the time, this blissful condition of complete desirelessness and non-attachment is the highest spiritual aspiration of the Buddhist path, commonly referred to as "nirvana." When following in the footsteps of Christ-Jesus, however, the condition of nirvana is discovered to be—not the culmination of the Christian path—but instead, the beginning of our Saviour's supersensible guidance into the spiritual world.[11]

2.5 Recognizing the Supersensible Voice of Christ-Jesus

On the Christian path into the spiritual world, the blissful repose in nirvana as one is about to consciously exit the lower bodies (for initiates and non-initiates alike) is a fleeting, temporal experience, not a condition of eternal rest. Once all personal thought activity has been stilled and one calmly abides in the trust of God, one's mind becomes more easily impressionable for the external benevolent forces and beings of the spiritual world.

As a result, the first thing that is most likely to break the non-initiate's brief nirvanic stillness of mind is a serene spirit-voice, calmly speaking with immense confidence and knowing-authority. This occurrence is crucially necessary when the non-initiate is exiting the physical body—especially for the first time—since they will need competent spirit-instruction and guidance in order to correctly and safely cross the threshold into the spiritual world..

What is wondrously amazing and mystifying to the unprepared non-initiate is the fact that the spirit-voice that is heard speaking with such knowing-authority is one's own inner voice. One is mysteriously listening to one's own superior advice and direction without willfully generating it.

When this occurs, though the non-initiate may be entirely unable to comprehend this baffling phenomenon, it is nevertheless welcomed with great relief, since this inner voice somehow seems to know exactly what to do and how to proceed—even though what is happening is entirely new and totally unfamiliar to the non-initiate.

Esoterically illuminated and explained, this guiding inner voice is simultaneously one's own voice *and* the voice of Christ-Jesus. Rather than authoritatively directing the non-initiate in an entirely external way, Christ-Jesus has chosen instead to transcendently raise up the non-initiate's own level of awareness to a more supernal degree of conscious knowing. As a wondrous consequence, the non-initiate is temporarily infused with a small degree of "Christ-consciousness," and thereby intuitively mirrors the all-wise direction of our Saviour for a brief period of time.

Moreover, by enabling the non-initiate to knowingly direct his or her own actions from a higher level of Christ-consciousness—rather than providing external direction through the force of his divine authority—Christ-Jesus better preserves the inviolable integrity of the non-initiate's free-will.

During the crucifixion experience, then, if the non-initiate has completely placed their trust in God and renounced all worldly attachments and desires, then they can be confident that from out of the stillness of nirvana God will respond by sending the "way-shower of mankind" as the voice of their own Christed-self to guide them across the threshold.

2.6 Following the Mystic Star

The initial instruction made by one's Christ-infused inner voice is to mentally concentrate all attention on a central point in the head directly between and behind the eyebrows; and then to focus exclusively on a tiny sun-burst of golden light that is situated there. While the non-initiate may already understand that the central point in the head is esoterically known as the "third-eye chakra,"[12] it is unlikely that they will have any prior knowledge of the golden point of light that is located there.

The non-initiate is unlikely to esoterically know that "I-consciousness" is supersensibly focalized in the centre of the brain where the pineal gland (and the third-eye chakra) is situated. Moreover, the spiritualized vehicles of expression that collectively constitute the "higher self"—spirit-self, life-spirit and spirit-body—are also anchored in this central locus of the brain (refer to Figure 1 on page 9 if necessary).

In most persons today (which includes non-initiates), the threefold vehicles of the higher-self continue to exist in an undeveloped, germinal condition. Consequently, spirit-self is clairvoyantly perceived as a small corona of bluish-violet light loosely surrounding the pineal (third-eye) gland. The life-spirit is perceived as an even smaller aureole of rose-pink light that closely envelopes the pineal centre. The spirit-body—the highest vehicle of expression possessed by human beings today—is in such a germinal condition that it only exists as a tiny sunburst of golden-white light at the very centre of the third-eye locus.[13]

Furthermore, this radiant point of golden light—known esoterically as the "mystic star"—most perfectly reflects the spirit of God for humanity today; and is thereby the germinal vehicle of divine consciousness. Directing the attention of the non-initiate to the mystic star during the crucifixion experience, therefore, truly elicits the divine guidance and assistance necessary to cross the threshold.

2.7 Exiting the Lower Bodies Through the Portal of the Third-Eye

Focusing on the mystic star as the soul is slowly exiting the etheric and physical bodies ensures that the non-initiate properly exits through the upper portal of the third-eye. In certain abnormal instances, the soul is deliberately or unknowingly forced to exit the physical and etheric bodies through a lower psychic-centre instead, such as the solar-plexus chakra situated in the navel region. Such an unfortunate practice is associated with black magic, and will certainly entrap the foolish soul in the malevolent regions of the lower-astral realm.

Following the advice of the Christed spirit-voice and the moving direction of the mystic God-star, the non-initiate—in a slow, spiraling movement—will safely rise up out of the lower bodies through the doorway of the third-eye. Moreover, since the non-initiate typically has undeveloped superphysical senses, it is unlikely that they will consciously perceive their astral body and ego-bearing soul vehicles during the out-of-body egress.

LESSON 3

TRAVERSING THE GREAT ABYSS

3.1 Encountering a Bottomless Chasm of Emptiness

UPON IMMEDIATELY EXITING the physical and etheric bodies, the non-initiate is, unfortunately, not greeted by a welcoming band of angels and joyously ushered into the heavenly realms. Instead, what confronts all those who seek to consciously enter the spiritual world is a yawning chasm of sheer unfathomable emptiness that stretches out indefinitely before one's paralyzed gaze.

Unfortunately for the untrained non-initiate, once the physical and etheric bodies have been vacated then all the familiar supports and foundations of material-solidity and earth-gravity disappear. In other words, in the superphysical realm, one can no longer stand on solid ground anymore. So to suddenly find oneself surrounded by emptiness, gazing at a bottomless pit below—with no physical means of support—is a terrifying introduction to consciously crossing the threshold.

3.2 Understanding the Great Abyss

Fortunately for trained initiates, they undergo repeatedly-rigorous mental and emotional preparation for the challenging encounter with the superphysical chasm of emptiness—known esoterically as the "great abyss." Initiates understand that the supersensible realm that is closest to the physical world is the etheric world. Moreover, similar to human persons, the planetary body of the earth is surrounded and interpenetrated by a number of superphysical vehicles or "meta-spheres"; such as an etheric meta-sphere, an astral meta-sphere and a soul meta-sphere (please refer to Figure 2 on page 20).

Also noteworthy is the esoteric fact that each of the meta-spheres of the earth is not of uniform consistency; but instead, there are coarser and finer gradations to each one. Typically, the closer the meta-sphere is to the centre of the earth, the coarser the gradation; and the further away the meta-sphere is from the earth, the finer the gradation.

Regarding the etheric meta-sphere of the earth, the subterranean gradations of etheric force and substance become increasingly dark, coarse, debased and corrupted toward the central core. Furthermore, highly-densified etheric substance exhibits a powerfully-centripetal, compressive action (similar to the scientific notion of a "black hole").

Contrarily, the gradations of etheric substance and force that extend outwardly toward the orbital circumference of the moon become increasingly luminous and radiant; exhibiting an elevatedly-expansive, centrifugal action (similar to the scientific notion of a "white hole"). As for the gradation of etheric force and substance that immediately surrounds the physical surface of the earth, in many respects it is characteristically neutral or empty—being neither coarse nor fine, neither dark nor light. Nevertheless, at this surface level it still retains an incessant absorbing action.

Regarding etheric substance, most non-initiates (and many esotericists) have an entirely erroneous understanding of its fundamental nature. The generally-accepted misconception is that the ether is simply ultra-refined physical matter, something akin to "rarified space." However surprising or startling it may seem, clairvoyantly-perceived ether is in reality emptier than empty space, a sort of "negative-space" or "counter-space." As explained by Rudolf Steiner in a lecture given on 16 April 1920 (and published in *Man: Hieroglyph of the Universe*; 1972):

> [E]mptier than empty space. This can be said of all parts of the Universe where we find Ether. For this reason it is so difficult for the physicist to speak of Ether, for he thinks that Ether is also matter, though more rarefied than ordinary matter …

> But in the transition from ponderable matter to Ether we have nothing to do with rarefaction … not only does matter become empty space, but it becomes negative, *less* than nothing—emptier than emptiness; it assumes a 'sucking' nature. Ether is sucking, absorbing. Matter *presses*. Ether *absorbs*.

From the foregoing, it can be better understood that the experience of the great abyss is essentially the out-of-body awareness of entering the etheric meta-sphere that immediately surrounds the surface of the earth. As indicated, this gradation of planetary ether is supersensibly perceived as a frightening chasm of total emptiness that appears to be horribly absorbing one into seeming oblivion.

3.3 The Great Abyss as the Boundary Between the Physical World and the Soul World

As diagrammatically illustrated in Figure 2, the etheric

plane exists midway between the material plane of the physical world and the lower astral plane of the soul world. Consequently, in order to pass from the material plane to the astral plane, it is unavoidably necessary to pass through the etheric plane. In other words, in order for the non-initiate to follow Christ-Jesus into the spiritual world, it is necessary to pass through—or "cross over"—the great abyss.

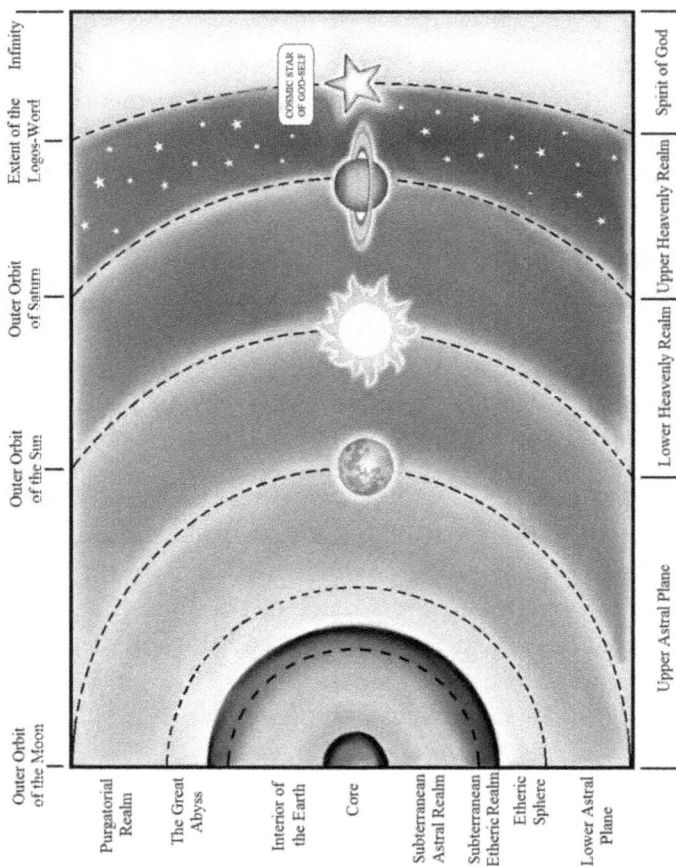

Figure 2: The Superphysical Regions of the Cosmos

3.4 The Necessity of Crossing the Great Abyss

As previously indicated in Lesson 1, in order for the non-initiate to safely follow Christ-Jesus into the spiritual world it is crucially necessary to confront and overcome the spectral apparition of their accumulated karmic evil prior to encountering the great abyss. If the lesser guardian of the threshold has not been previously subdued, then at the very moment of attempting to pass through the terrifying boundary of superphysical emptiness, the powerful emotional forces of fear, doubt and hatred rise up out of the subterranean ethers to block any forward passage.

Since etheric substance has the innate tendency to easily metamorphosize into innumerable shapes, figures, pictures and images, the negative emotional obstacles of fear, doubt and hatred appear out of the etheric abyss as horrifying spectral creatures (see note 5). Unfortunately for the unprepared non-initiate, these spectrally-personified emotions will pull them down into the torpid abyss; thereby extinguishing their self-awareness, and inducing the unconsciousness of deep sleep.

Interestingly, the challenge of crossing the great abyss has been metaphorically illustrated in the gospel of Matthew (14:26–34):

> When evening came ... the boat by this time was many furlongs distant from the land, beaten by the waves; for the wind was against them ... But when the disciples saw him walking on the sea, they were terrified, saying, "It is a ghost!" ... But immediately he spoke to them, saying, "Take heart, it is I; have no fear." And Peter answered him, "Lord, if it is you, bid me come to you on the water." He said, "Come." So Peter got out of the boat and walked on the water and came to Jesus; but when he saw the wind, he was afraid, and beginning to sink he cried out, "Lord, save me." Jesus immediately reached out

his hand and caught him, saying to him, "O man of little faith, why did you doubt?" ... And when they had crossed over, they came to land at Gennesaret.

This biblical passage can be esoterically interpreted to say that "when evening came" (*when Jesus' disciples were asleep*) and "distant from land" (*and out of their physical bodies*), "the disciples saw him walking on the sea" (*the disciples clairvoyantly perceived Christ-Jesus levitating over the great abyss*) "saying, 'It is a ghost'" (*appearing to them in his astral form*).

"And Peter answered him, "Lord, if it is you, bid me come to you on the water" (*Peter—the typical non-initiate—asked for Christ's assistance to also cross the great abyss*). "So Peter got out of the boat and walked on the water" (*Then Peter entered the great abyss*); "but when he saw the wind, he was afraid, and beginning to sink" (*but when he was overtaken by fear coming from the guardian of the threshold, Peter began to descend into the abyss*).

"Jesus immediately reached out his hand and caught him, saying to him, 'O man of little faith, why did you doubt?' (*Christ-Jesus' instruction to safely cross the abyss was to overcome fear and doubt with faith and trust in God*). "And when they had crossed over, they came to land at Gennesaret" (*and when they had successfully crossed the great abyss, then they entered the astral realm*).

3.5 The Divine Protection of the Mystic Star

For the typical non-initiate with no prior knowledge of the great abyss, it is highly unlikely that they will know how to consciously traverse the yawning chasm of etheric emptiness. As with properly exiting the physical body, the wisest course of action (as indicated in the biblical event interpreted above) is to continue to have "faith in God"; that is, maintain exclusive mental focus on the golden point of light—the mystic star of inner God-consciousness—that continues to steadily shine within the globally-surrounding sphere of suctioning emptiness.

When encountering the terrifying abyss, the non-initiate can be assured that authoritative instruction from their own higher Christ-self will calmly direct them to focus their entire attention on the mystic star. In other words, out of superior higher-wisdom, the non-initiate will knowingly instruct him or herself on exactly what to do in this crucial situation.

What unexpectedly occurs as an immediate result is the formation of a protective sphere or "bubble" of golden light which completely surrounds the non-initiate. Within this luminous cocoon, the non-initiate is protectively ferried across the great abyss. But unfortunately, the observant non-initiate will note that their quick and safe passage through the great emptiness is not in an upward direction, but in a gradually descending one.

Moreover, unbeknownst to the intrepid non-initiate the far side of the great abyss is not the heavenly shores of the spiritual world; but instead, the gateway into the subterranean, lower-astral sphere of planet earth. If the entry into the planetary etheric-sphere can be described as "soul-terrifying," the subsequent entry into the debased, subterranean astral-sphere can be described as "soul-shattering."

LESSON 4:

DESCENDING INTO HELL

4.1   Penetrating the Tectonic Crust of the Earth

IT IS HUGELY DISCONCERTING for the unprepared non-initiate to discover that even after being safely ferried across the vast, seemingly-bottomless abyss, there is no resting place; nor is there a joyful entry through the gates of paradise. Instead, one begins to experience a gradual descending motion that begins to accelerate. What occurs next is entirely unexpected, unfamiliar, unforeseeable, and completely terrorizing.

One crashingly plummets headlong into a thunderously-deafening, subterranean planetary layer of rock-crushing, stone-grinding, earth-shattering tectonic upheaval of enormous crustal plates; below which is a seething, convulsing planetary layer of fiery, magmatic volcanization.

In life-threatening fear of being soul-crushingly annihilated, one may be instinctually driven to cry out: "Lord save me!" Thankfully, by the grace of God, the non-initiate continues to be miraculously protected by the enveloping sphere of golden light; and in consequence, passes unscathed relatively quickly through these violent layers of planetary destruction.

During this horrifying out-of-body experience, it is unlikely that many non-initiates will understand that after passing through the etheric sphere that surrounds the earth (the abyss), they are impelled to enter—not the higher—but the degenerate, lower-astral region of the planet that superphysically lies beneath the surface.

4.2 Mythological Journeys to the Underworld

Many of the ancient mythologies clearly indicate that our distant ancestors were well aware that crossing the threshold during initiation or after death entailed a harrowing "journey to the underworld," instead of an immediate entry into the realms of paradisal bliss.[14]

While these chthonic journeys were usually undertaken by the souls of the dead, on rare occasions it was intrepid travelers from the land of the living—heroes, mystics or shamans—who undertook the terrifying, dangerous and unpredictable journey. Moreover, many of these mythic, underworld journeys also entailed the need to cross over, or through, some difficult obstacle—such as a baleful lake or malevolent river—before entering the shadowy and mysterious underworld.

In many ancient mythologies, *every* soul journeyed to the underworld after death; while in other myths, it was only the souls of the damned that were condemned to the underworld as punishment for an evil life on earth. It was also commonly held that even though the underworld existed below the earth's surface and could be secretly accessed by descending into a deep well, pit, or cavern—it was nevertheless a supernatural realm; and the abode of other numinous creatures and beings (such as demons, fairies, elementals and ghostly-sprites).

In ancient Mesopotamian mythology, for example, the underworld (as described in the epic of Gilgamesh) was a desiccated, shadowy and gloomy place called the House of Darkness. Unable to escape, the pale and spectral souls of the dead dwelt in darkness, feeding only on dust and clay.

Likewise, to the ancient Hebrews, the underworld was a similar place of darkness called Sheol (meaning "grave," "pit" or "abyss"); and it was originally believed to contain the souls of every person who had lived on earth—good and bad. Only later did Sheol become a specific place of torment and punishment for sinners.

The underworld in ancient Greek mythology was also a stygian and wraithlike realm deep within the earth where departed souls moved about as phantasmal "shades." The Grecian underworld was believed to be separated from the land of the living by five subterranean rivers: Acheron (woe), Styx (hate), Lethe (forgetfulness), Cocytus (wailing), and Phlegethon (fire). Moreover, the entrance to the underworld was further protected by a fierce, three-headed, doglike beast known as Cerberus.

The Grecian underworld also consisted of three regions—one being Hades (after the god who ruled over it), where most souls were confined; a second being Elysium or the Elysian Fields, where dwelt the souls of the righteous; and a third being a deep, dark pit called Tartarus, where the souls of the wicked were eternally tormented by creatures called Furies.

In ancient Mayan mythology, the underworld was an even more hideous, subterranean realm known as Xibalba, which meant "place of fear." All departed souls journeyed to Xibalba—except those who had already died a violent death. Xibalba was ruled by 12 death gods who meted out ghastly punishments by working in pairs. Their names were a horrid indication of their gruesome tasks: such as Pus Master, Bone Sceptre, Jaundice Master and Blood Gatherer.

Xibalba had nine levels of horrific torment where departed souls were forced to undergo blood-curdling ordeals—such as crossing a river of scorpions, a river of blood and a river of pus—after which they endured a house of ferocious jaguars, an assault from slashing, spinning razors, and then a scalding from an unquenchable fire.

Perhaps no other ancient culture was more obsessed with the details of life after death than the Egyptian. As with all the other ancient cultures mentioned thus far, Egyptian mythology believed that immediately after death, all souls—including the souls of their god-kings, the pharaohs—travelled to Duat, the supernatural underworld beneath the surface of the earth.

To enter the Egyptian underworld, it was necessary to be ferried across a formidable river by a creature with eyes in the back of its head. Once in Duat, the souls of the dead had to successfully pass through 12 levels or chambers populated with terrifying demons and monsters; as well as several impenetrable gates that were lined with sharp spears and guarded by venomous, fire-breathing serpents.

It was only after surviving these violent and brutal ordeals that the persevering soul was permitted to enter the kingdom of Osirus, the lord of the dead. It was here that deceased souls faced divine judgement by having their hearts weighed against the feather of Ma'at, the goddess of truth and justice. A heart weighed down with evil was devoured by Ammut, a demoness that was part lion, crocodile and hippo. A righteous heart that was "light as a feather" went on to eternally live with the gods in an underworld paradise.

While numerous other mythologies could be further described to indicate the widespread knowledge in ancient times that crossing the threshold into the spiritual world (after death or in life) begins with a journey to the underworld, only one more will be touched on here—Norse mythology. This is simply to indicate that the most commonly used word for the underworld—hell—is derived from a Norse goddess named Hel, who ruled over an underworld kingdom of the same name (also called Helheim).

The word Hel means "hidden place," and according to the Norse book *Gylfaginning*, it was a dark, cold and joyless place where "evil men" go after death. In order to enter the gates of Hel, it was necessary to travel for nine nights, then cross a "noisy" river and a "furiously guarded" bridge.

4.3 Falling Through the Dark Interior of the Earth

After crashing through the sub-surface layer of violent crustal upheaval, and the fiery, molten, magmatic layer beneath, the plummet downwards will horrifyingly continue for the understandably-confused non-initiate. Since non-initiates are typically unprepared for such a sub-earthly descent, this soul-shattering experience can be terrifyingly perceived as an eternal banishment to hell. After having placed one's entire trust in God during the crucifixion ordeal, the feeling of uncontrollably plunging into hell will understandably illicit an agonized cry from the non-initiate, such as: "My God, my God; why have you forsaken me!"

Since the non-initiate, by definition, has not developed his or her superphysical soul-senses through initiatory training, the supernatural perception of the earth's interior will be somewhat limited. Moreover, when following Christ across the threshold, it is only through the temporary, grace-filled infusion of Christ-consciousness that the non-initiate is able to remain fully conscious with even limited clairvoyant perception.

As the non-initiate continues to descend deeper and deeper into the earth, the perceptual experience is typically one of passing through several layers of increasing darkness; accompanied by a suffocating feeling of increasing external oppression. Thankfully nonetheless, even though the superphysical underworld is esoterically known to be teeming with numerous inimical, demonic and destructive entities (such as asuras[15] and ahrimanic beings[16]), the non-initiate is unlikely to perceive them since that requires a much more advanced supersensory development.[17]

4.4 The Interior of the Earth According to Empirical Science

Obviously, as a supernatural experience, the interior of the earth will not be perceived physically; that is, as empirical science has determined. Geologically, the earth's interior is described as consisting of four layers: the crust, the mantle, the outer core and the inner core (please refer to Figure 3 on the following page for diagrammatic illustration).

The crust is the outermost and thinnest layer of the physical earth; ranging in thickness from about eight kilometers beneath the oceans, to an average of 25 kilometers beneath the continents. Also, the crust is not a uniform and continuous geophysical "skin" surrounding the earth; but is fractured instead into a number of slowly-moving, gigantic crustal-plates that collide with each other over time, tossing up vast mountain ranges and causing earthquakes.

The layer beneath the outer crust is known as the mantle; and with a thickness of 2900 kilometers, it is clearly the largest geophysical layer in the earth's interior making up around 85% of the planet's volume. The mantle is believed to be composed of very hot silicate rock in a viscous, semi-solid fluid condition. Even though the temperature of the mantle ranges from 300° Celsius near the crust to 4500° Celsius near the outer core, it is prevented from fully melting and liquefying due to the tremendous lithostatic pressure within the earth.

Beneath the mantle is the earth's core, which geophysical science divides into two distinct layers: an outer core and an inner core. Rather than rock, both the outer and inner core are believed to be composed almost entirely of metal; particularly iron with substantial amounts of nickel and sulphur.

Being metal rather than rock, the outer layer of the core is able to liquefy from the 4000° to 5000° Celsius temperature, despite the enormous pressure. The white-hot inner core, however, even though the 5000° to 7000° Celsius temperature approximates the surface of the sun, is unable to liquefy because of the overwhelming pressure at the heart of the planet.

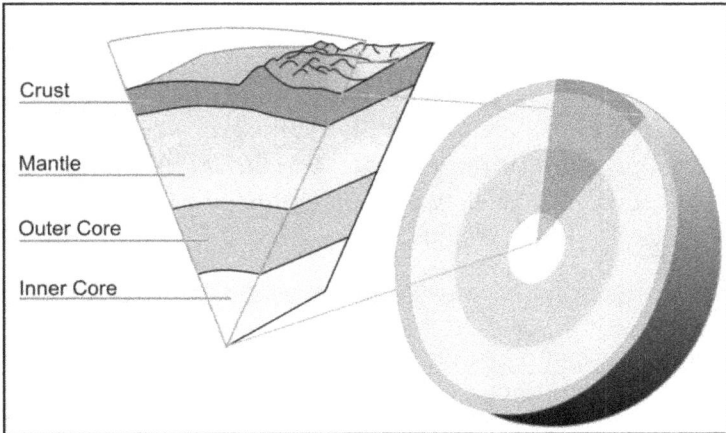

Figure 3: The Geophysical Interior of the Earth (not to scale)

When supernaturally descending into the earth's interior, obviously perception will be different than that of the physical senses. While the initial out-of-body crashing through the crustal surface of the earth is perceived somewhat similarly to geophysical observation, thankfully there is no sensation of skin-searing physical heat or bone-crushing physical pressure when supersensibly descending into the earth.

4.5 The Interior of the Earth According to Spiritual Science

It is not surprising that the non-initiate's perception of the earth's superphysical (not geophysical) interior will be experientially limited, since the very highest attainment of clairvoyant ability is required to penetrate super-densified and debased subterranean matter. It is far easier, even for trained initiates, to clairvoyantly perceive the higher heavenly realms than it is to gaze even an inch below the earth's surface.

Even a highly-advanced Rosicrucian initiate such as Rudolf Steiner had great difficulty clairvoyantly perceiving the underworld realm of the earth. In a lecture given on 16 April 1906, entitled "The Interior of the Earth and Volcanic Eruptions," Steiner stated the following:

> [E]ven among occultists it is considered one of the most difficult things to speak about, the mysterious configuration and composition of our planet earth ... it is easier to gain a living experience of the astral and mental worlds, of kamaloka and devachan, and to bring it to ordinary day-consciousness than it is to penetrate the secrets of our own planet earth. In point of fact, these secrets are among the 'inner secrets' which are reserved for a higher grade, the second grade, of initiation. No one has, to date, spoken in public about the interior of the earth, not even within the theosophical movement.

In spite of the extreme clairvoyant difficulty involved, Rudolf Steiner did manage to reveal some astoundingly-unusual and totally-original detail regarding the superphysical interior of the earth. For instance, the subterranean earth is supersensibly observed to have nine distinct layers or strata: the Mineral-Earth, the Fluid-Earth, the Vapour-Earth, the Water-Earth, the Fruit-Earth, the Fire-Earth, the Mirror-Earth, the Fragmentor-Earth, and the Ego-Centric Egotism-Core (please refer to Figure 4 on page 34 for diagrammatic illustration).

Once again, it's important to keep in mind that these particular subterranean layers are superphysical, and not physical. Just as the human physical body is interpenetrated by vehicles of soul and spirit, so is the planetary geophysical body interpenetrated by spheres of soul and spirit. Only the top layer of Mineral-Earth can be observed and described geophysically. As described by Rudolf Steiner:

> As the human body is filled with soul and spirit, so is the body of the whole body of the earth filled with soul and spirit. And just as the blood consists not only of chemical compounds chemists are able to identify, so specific substances and layers of our earth are far from being only what metallurgists, crystallographers and chemists are able to discover. Just as the nerves are not merely the anatomical structures defined by scientists, having special significance in expressing soul structures, so too there is an aspect of soul and spirit to everything that makes up our earth. (Ibid)

The second layer of Fluid-Earth, then, is nor fluid in a physical sense; but rather in a densified etheric sense—something akin to rarified matter. As such it can be partially perceived with the physical senses. However, it is a deadly sphere of negative life that dissolves and extinguishes anything that is alive. It also has an inherent tendency to rapidly expand and shatter apart when not super-contained within the earth's protective interior.

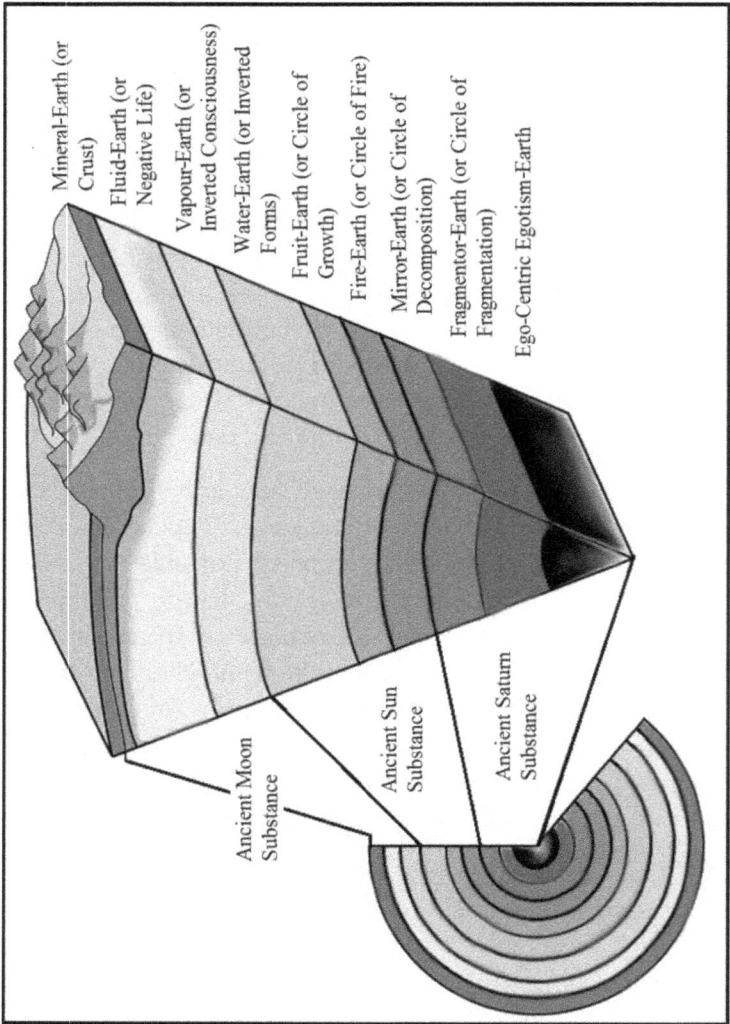

Figure 4: The Superphysical Interior of the Earth

The third layer of Vapour-Earth is likewise a sphere of densified etheric-astral material; not physical water vapour, for example. Nevertheless, in its super-compressed state it bears some resemblance to physical matter. As the second layer was best characterized as negative life, the third layer is best characterized as negative emotion, or inverted consciousness. A feeling of joy, for example, will be inverted into sorrow. Where there is the negation of life in the second subterranean layer, then, there is the negative reversal of emotion in the third layer.

The fourth layer of Water-Earth does not, of course, refer to physical water; but rather the mutable, mobile nature of debased astral material. This atavistic primal substance was once the source of later-densified physical matter; but in its original uncondensed state it is only perceptible clairvoyantly. Within this layer, forms undergo a kind of "space reversal." The internal space that a form would normally fill with substance becomes hollowed out and emptied. Instead of filling the form, then, the internal substance becomes externally spread around the empty space of the form.

In Rosicrucian terminology, the fifth esoteric layer of the earth is referred to as the Fruit-Earth; since the teeming energies of archetypical growth in this layer once brought primitive life-forms to "fruition" in the primordial past of the earth.

The sixth supersensible layer of the earth is termed the Fire-Earth. "Fire" in this case does not, of course, refer to physical fire; but instead to fiery, atavistic passions, impulses and will-forces that characteristically permeate this primeval subterranean layer. Furthermore, what is of crucial significance regarding the Fire-Earth is the esoteric knowledge that the exercise of human will has a strong, psychic connection and affinity with the degenerate will-forces of this deep subterranean layer. Consequently, evil expressions of human-will correspondingly result in disruptions within the Fire-Earth; to the point that serious disturbances from widespread evil have historically resulted in fiery volcanic cataclysms on the earth's surface (the destruction of ancient Lemuria, for example).[18]

The seventh subterranean layer, termed the Mirror-Earth, is suffused with degenerate primeval forces of nature that possess a depraved, corrupting component. As such, this nefarious layer reflects or "mirrors" all positive natural force into its debauched immoral opposite.

The Fragmentor-Earth, as the eighth layer, is so-called because the degenerate forces within this sphere will fracture, splinter and fragment countless distorted copies of any life-form or human creation (such as a work of art).

The ninth layer is the debased core of the planet, and is esoterically termed the Ego-Centric Egotism-Earth. The primeval, degenerate substance at the planetary centre is sated with a depraved and dissolute sexuality. As such, the dark forces of the ninth sphere are entirely resistant to moral goodness and virtue; and are the subterranean source of black magical power on earth.

4.6 Going Backward in Time by Descending Inward

As the non-initiate continues to plummet ever deeper into the earth's interior, with only the limited clairvoyant perception infused by Christ, there will be little sensory notice of the various layers that are described by spiritual science. Instead, the non-initiate is more likely to experience a growing feeling of moral darkness and evil; as well as an increased feeling of suffocating soul-constriction.

Not knowing exactly what is happening or what will occur next, the terrified non-initiate's best course of action is to continue having complete and total trust and faith in God. Without fail, this child-like spiritual dependency will continue to re-invoke the calming voice of one's own Christ-self to remain focused on the golden point of light in the distance ahead; that is, to concentrate on the mysteriously-moving mystic star that appears to be guiding one forward in some strangely-inexorable way.

What is also very likely to occur as the non-initiate continues to plummet into the dark substratal unknown is the fearful feeling of travelling backwards in time—back to the primal beginning of cosmic life. One is likely to conclude from this disconcerting experience that one is either dying, or already dead.

What the non-initiate is unlikely to realize at the time, is that the experience of hurtling backwards in time as one sinks deeper into the earth's interior is entirely consistent with the earth's supersensible interior as described by spiritual science.[19] The nine subterranean layers are all understood to be densified atavistic matter and energy from previous primordial stages in earth development.[20] The top three layers are detritus from the Ancient Moon Period; the middle three layers are debris from the Ancient Sun Period; and the innermost three layers are offal from the Ancient Saturn Period (please refer to Figure 4 on page 34 for diagrammatic illustration).

By descending deeper and deeper into the earth, then, the non-initiate is indeed travelling back through the increasingly older and increasingly more primitive stages in earth development—even to degenerate matter and energy from the very inception of our current solar system. While this primordial matter and energy was progressive and evolutionary during these ancient developmental stages, in our current planetary period they are atavistic, archaic, degenerate and harmful. And of course, the more primeval the matter and energy, the more debased, degraded and destructive they are to present-day life on earth. The earth's core, then, is the crudest, most deleterious, most nocuous and most dangerous layer of the entire planet. Fortunately, all these life-destroying layers from the primeval past have all been safely contained within the earth's interior by the powerful spiritual beings who progressively guide human and earthly evolution.

4.7 Journeying Deeper into the "Bowels" of the Earth

Coincident with the perception that one is collapsing backwards in time toward some cosmic genesis-point of life is the additional disconcerting impression that one is descending deeper into the literal "bowels" of the earth. One has the disturbing feeling of penetrating further and further into some organic-like abdominal region deep within the earth.

Once again, this seemingly-implausible and inexplicable experience is confirmed and explained by spiritual-scientific research:

> One can only say that one becomes aware how specific parts of the interior of the earth have a certain relationship to individual organs of human and animal bodies ... Still further inside this sphere are forces connected with human and animal powers of reproduction. (Ibid)

LESSON 5:

REACHING THE INFERNAL CORE
OF THE EARTH

5.1 The Descent into the Underworld Comes to a Halt

HAVING NEVER CONSCIOUSLY experienced a journey into the planetary underworld before, the terrified non-initiate—despite putting their entire trust in God—doesn't necessarily know if the downward plunge into deeper and deeper layers of subterranean darkness will ever stop; or will it continue for all eternity; or will their very existence be annihilated in some unknown way?

Fortunately, the accelerating descent suddenly comes to an abrupt halt. Unfortunately, however, the unexpected landing is within a horrible sphere of primeval matter at the centre of the earth. It's not unusual, then, for the terrified non-initiate to shudderingly feel that for some horrible reason, they have "gone to hell."

5.2 Ancient, Decadent Matter and Energy at the Earth's Core

Unless the non-initiate is familiar with the spiritual-scientific perception of the earth's interior (as illustrated in Figure 4), then it would be extremely unlikely to be mentally and emotionally prepared for the horrifying experience within the earth's core. Thankfully, with only limited clairvoyant ability, there is likely to be no sense of smell, or touch, or taste—only sight and sound. The sight, however, is truly ghastly to behold; and completely foreign to any comparable experience on the surface above.

At this point in the journey, the non-initiate is repulsively surrounded by loathsomely-degenerate and debased matter anachronistically retained from some ancient cosmic evolution. To clairvoyant sight, the degraded flesh-coloured substance writhes and convulses from some primitive, serpentine life-force within it. As well as being horribly alive to the inner-sight, this primeval convolution rumbles, groans, growls and gurgles in a deep, brutish, intestinal chorus.

While it is certainly understandable for the non-initiate to temporarily lose sight of the fact—given such repugnant surroundings—they continue to remain divinely-protected within the transparent sphere of golden Christ-light that originally ferried them across the abyss. Nevertheless, it is still frightfully uncertain at the time whether this infernal domain is eternally permanent or not; hence the importance of remaining fixed on the guiding mystic star.

5.3 The Centre of the Earth as the Infernal Domain of Sorath the Sun-Demon

Thank God (in a literal sense) that the unprepared non-initiate is only infused with *limited* clairvoyance throughout the journey into the underworld. As a result, only forms, shapes, colours, light, darkness and movement are discernible; as well as some basic sounds. To supersensibly perceive spiritual beings, a much more advanced clairvoyant ability is required.

Since the subterranean lower-astral realm is the abode of powerfully-destructive and inimical spirit-beings, it is indeed a blessing that the non-initiate is unable to confront them directly; but is instead only able to perceive their corrupting effects on sub-astral matter and energy. Consequently, when falling through the sub-layer of Fire-Earth, the malevolently-evil being Ahriman/Satan is not perceived, even though this layer is his primary base of activity.[21]

In conventional Christianity, Ahriman/Satan has been traditionally known as the devil, the ruler over the realm of the damned, known as hell. To spiritual science, however, the devil's region (the sixth layer of Fire-Earth) is only a little more than midway into the underworld. Far deeper into hell, at the core of the planetary underworld, is imprisoned a far more powerful and ancient evil-being known esoterically as Sorath, the sun-demon.

In St. John's biblical book of Revelation, Sorath is referred to as the two-horned beast who arises out of the earth, and whose number is 666.[22] Moreover, Sorath is esoterically known to be a powerfully-evil intruder from an evolutionary system far more distant and much, much older than our own. And for some egotistically-malicious reason of his own, Sorath's evil intent is to assume complete control over our entire solar system. Consequently, the sun-demon has declared himself the arch-enemy of the true leader of our sun system—the Solar-Christos (ie: the Christ-Being).

Although Sorath can't be directly perceived by the non-initiate, his evil influence on the atavistic matter and energy of the earth's core can certainly be gut-wrenchingly felt. Even a non-initiate can clairvoyantly sense a black-magical seduction and a perverse-sexual allurement exuding from the florid, incessantly-writhing and coiling serpentine-substance at the earth's core.

5.4 The Regurgitation of Debased Matter at the Centre of the Earth

As with every event thus far, when consciously following Christ across the threshold, what occurs next for the non-initiate in hell—the debased core of the earth—is entirely inconceivable, unimaginable, unforeseeable and totally horrifying. Just as one is beginning to fearfully conclude that they may have been cast into hell forever, the convulsing, intertwining flesh-like substance suddenly "disgorges" itself! In a sickeningly-audible regurgitation, the infernal astral-matter in the core seems to somehow turn itself inside out!

In addition, this rapid internal retching acts as an expelling force that propels the totally-surprised non-initiate upwards and out of the hell-sphere of the earth.

LESSON 6:

THE TRIUMPHANT ASCENT FROM HELL AND FLIGHT INTO SPACE

6.1 Rising Upward Toward the Planetary Surface

WHILE IT IS EXTREMELY difficult to convey in words the horrific experience of sojourning in hell (even for a brief time), it is equally demanding to somehow convey in words the unbounded, jubilant elation of rising upwards out of hell toward the surface of the earth once again.

Instead of fearfully falling deeper and deeper into oppressive spiritual darkness, the non-initiate now experiences him or herself ecstatically rising higher and higher toward uplifting spiritual light. The feeling is comparable to an unfortunate swimmer who becomes trapped in deep water and in danger of drowning; who then suddenly becomes free to rise upwards toward the sunlit surface, desperately gasping for air.

As the horrifying plummet downward into the underworld seemed to accelerate for the non-initiate, the exuberant soaring upward also seems to increase in speed. As well, the previously-dark subterranean layers now appear to become lighter and brighter. The welcoming surface-layer of the planet becomes a translucent etheric-window revealing a shining, sky-blue world beyond.

6.2 Breaking Through the Surface of the Earth

It would be logical to expect that after having survived—by the grace of God—the terrifying descent into the hellish underworld, and having re-ascended to the planetary surface, the non-initiate would return to their sleeping physical body and awaken. But once again, there is little predictability to following Christ across the threshold into the spiritual world. Instead of simply returning to ordinary surface life, the exultant non-initiate continues to exhilaratingly soar above and beyond the surface of the earth.

Instead of fearfully descending into the degraded lower-astral realm *within* the earth, the jubilant non-initiate now ascends into the lower-astral sphere that outwardly extends *beyond* the surface of the earth to the orbital circumference of the moon (please refer to Figure 2). Even though the earth's lower-astral sphere is the superphysical realm of the angelic hierarchy, the limited clairvoyance of the non-initiate is unable to directly perceive their presence. Nevertheless, as the non-initiate continues to soar higher and higher above and beyond the surface of the earth, there is no fear of heights or sense of threatening doom, only an increasing sense of superterrestrial freedom.

6.3 Liberatingly Rising Above the Earth

Esoterically, the lower-astral sphere that surrounds the earth is also referred to as "purgatory."[23] This designation is used because, within this realm after death, discarnate souls immersively recall their previous lives on earth; and thereby intensely experience the pain or joy that their actions have caused to others. By doing so, souls are karmically "purged" or purified of their earthly misdeeds; and thus are better able to leave earthly attachments and constraints behind to ascend into the heaven worlds.

In the case of the non-initiate who is following Christ across the threshold into the spiritual world, they have already completely renounced all earthly captivations and allurements during their crucifixion experience. Consequently, there is no psychic restraint or resistance as they sail easily and effortlessly through the lower-astral, purgatorial realm.

6.4 Joyously Soaring Outwardly into Planetary Space

Once again it would be quite logical to expect that after rising a short distance above the earth, the non-initiate would safely return to the planetary surface and to their waiting physical body. On the contrary, however, the non-initiate unpredictably continues to acceleratingly soar farther and farther out into planetary space.

Even though the non-initiate is unlikely to have ever consciously experienced out-of-body space-travel before, unlike the descent into the underworld, there are no feelings of fear or terror associated with this occurrence—only unbounded exhilaration and joy. Surprisingly, it matters not "why" the astral space-flight is occurring?; or "where" it is leading?; or "how long" it will last?; or even "what" will happen next? In this case, complete faith and trust in God appears to be joyfully leading in God's direction.

Since the discarnate non-initiate is experiencing this planetary journey with clairvoyant perception, the individual planets do not appear as they would with physical sense-perception. Rather than appearing as three-dimensional spherical bodies suspended in space, they appear as diffuse and interpenetrating realms of superphysical light and colour. Passing through the lunar realm that surrounds the earth, for example, is like sailing through a planetary ocean of shimmering, silver moonlight.

To the clairvoyant sight of the non-initiate, then, soaring farther and farther away from the earth is not experienced as a frightening journey into the dark void of deep-space. Instead, it's an exhilarating odyssey through planetary spheres of varying light and colour. By continuing to remain steadfastly focused on the golden-white spark of their God-self (the mystic star), after sailing through the silvery, lower-astral sphere of the moon, the non-initiate is subsequently guided through the luminous, upper-astral spheres of Venus and Mercury toward the golden effulgence of the sun.

Passing beyond the dazzling sphere of the sun toward the lower-heavenly reaches of the solar system engenders an indescribable sense of limitless freedom and carefree abandon. It's as though the entire cosmos opens out to the non-initiate in a welcoming embrace. Whereas the descent into the dark underworld couldn't end fast enough for the terrified non-initiate, the astral-flight into cosmic space feels like an experience that could happily continue for all eternity. Nevertheless, once the orbital circumference of Saturn is reached, the outward acceleration into deep-space takes a surprising turn.

6.5 Going Backward in Time by Expanding into Space

Since empirical science now acknowledges that our present universe is expanding, it is also understood that the farther out into space we observe from the earth, the further back in time we go. So for example, if we observe a star one million light-years away, we are actually observing that star as it was one million years ago; since it took that length of time for the starlight to reach the earth.

It is similarly understood in spiritual science that the farther away from the earth we travel in planetary space, the further back in time we go through the remnant conditions of previous evolutionary stages of the solar system. In other words, when the non-initiate travels outwardly through the successive spheres of the moon, sun and Saturn, they are in turn travelling back through the anachronistic residues of the Ancient Moon Period, the Ancient Sun Period and the Ancient Saturn Period of our solar system's evolutionary history (please refer to Figure 2).

The experience of travelling back in time through planetary space is, however, far different than travelling back in time through the subterranean earth. In the case of the planetary underworld, the atavistic matter and energy from primordial evolutionary periods has been further corrupted and debased by the malevolent beings within the earth (such as Ahriman and Sorath). The result is that travelling back in time through the sub-astral underworld is experienced as a terrifying return to a depraved and degenerate cosmic beginning that didn't actually exist.

However, in the case of travelling back in time through planetary space, since the non-initiate is moving through higher levels of superphysical existence (such as the higher-astral and lower-heavenly planes), the experience is one of soaring back in time to the divine inception of the universe. By faithfully following the mystic star of their divine-self into planetary space, the non-initiate ecstatically feels that they are being somehow drawn back in time to the God of all creation.

6.6 The Planetary "Switching-Station" of Saturn

Even though the non-initiate may be joyously content to continue travelling God-ward through cosmic space, upon reaching the lower-heavenly sphere of Saturn they are suddenly and forcefully spun around, and hurled back toward the earth. It appears that Saturn acts as some sort of planetary "switching station" to prevent non-deceased astral-travelers from continuing farther out into space; and thereby prevent them from entering the upper-heavenly realm.

It's easy to envision that the characteristic ring-formation around the physical planet is a dense, material manifestation of the superphysical, centripetal function of the Saturn sphere. No doubt this impelling operation is connected with the esoteric fact that the orbital circumference of Saturn defines the outer reach of our original solar system. Uranus, Neptune and Pluto are considered to be later planetary acquisitions.[24]

.

LESSON 7:

ENCOUNTERING CHRIST IN THE SPHERE OF THE SUN

7.1 A Brief Sojourn Within the Golden Radiance of the Sun

EVEN THOUGH THE NON-INITIATE is involuntarily hurled back to earth by the superphysical centripetal forces of Saturn, the astral flight is no less exhilarating or predictable. Whereas the non-initiate's outward flight sailed blissfully unimpeded through the sphere of the sun, on the return flight back to earth a brief but supremely-profound sojourn occurs.

Since the non-initiate throughout the intrepid journey across the threshold has continued to faithfully focus on the guiding mystic star of their divine-self, Christ-Jesus has reciprocatingly infused them with limited clairvoyance, provided them with transcendently-wise instruction, and surrounded them with luminous psychic protection.

Having safely passed through the frighteningly-dark underworld and successfully journeyed to the very edge of the solar system, the soul of the non-initiate is now experientially prepared to encounter Christ—the exalted Solar-Christos—in the realm of the sun. But once again, due to limited clairvoyant perception, the full majesty and sublime-being of the Solar-Christos is not directly encountered; but indirectly experienced instead.

7.2 Understanding Christ as the Exalted Solar-Christos

Unless the non-initiate is familiar with the spiritual-scientific research of Rudolf Steiner, it is unlikely that they will understand the superphysical connection of Christ-Jesus with the sun. Even though our Saviour biblically declared: "I am the light of the world" (Jn 8:12), this is traditionally understood to be an exclusive reference to the *divine* light of God; without any associated reference to the physical and spiritual light of the sun.

According to esoteric tradition and modern-day spiritual science, the word "Christ" does not simply confer the title of "Messiah" on Jesus; but also refers to an illustrious celestial being whose supernal centre of activity is the numinous sphere of the sun. Esoterically known as the Solar-Christos, this celestial being is a highly-advanced fire-spirit (or archangel) who functions at the level of a virtue (or spirit of motion). As such, Christ the Solar-Christos is the eminent leader of all the solar-spirits—the celestial beings who invisibly dwell in the superphysical sphere of the sun (please refer to Figure 5 on the next page).

In addition, spiritual-scientific research asserts that at the baptism of Jesus in the Jordan River, Christ the Solar-Christos infused him with supernatural power; thereby raising his conscious awareness up to God the Son. In other words, Jesus, through infused Christ-consciousness, became united (or "one") with the Son. Thereafter, he becomes known as "Christ-Jesus, the son of God."[25]

	WESTERN THEOLOGY	HEBREW TRADITION	GREEK TRADITION	ANTHROPOSOPHY
THE TRIUNE GOD	THE BLESSED TRINITY (INCLUDES)	YAHWEH	THEOS	THE TRINITY
THE WORD	THE WORD	MEMRA	LOGOS	THE CREATIVE WORD
FIRST HIERARCHY	SERAPHIM	CHAIOTH HA-QADESH	(SERAPHIM)	SPIRITS OF LOVE
	CHERUBIM	AUPHANIM	(CHERUBIM)	SPIRITS OF HARMONY
	THRONES	CHASHMALIM	(THRONES)	SPIRITS OF WILL
SECOND HIERARCHY	DOMINIONS	SERAPHIM	KYRIOTETES	SPIRITS OF WISDOM
	VIRTUES	MALACHIM	DYNAMEIS	SPIRITS OF MOVEMENT
	POWERS	ELOHIM	EXUSIAI	SPIRITS OF FORM
THIRD HIERARCHY	PRINCIPALITIES	BENE ELOHIM	ARCHAI	TIME SPIRITS
	ARCHANGELS	KERUBIM	ARCHANGELOI	SUN SPIRITS
	ANGELS	ISHIM	ANGELOI	MOON SPIRITS
	HUMANITY	BENEI-ADAM	ANTHROPOS	SPIRITS OF FREEDOM

Figure 5: The Universal Hierarchy of Being

7.3 Being Infused with Christ-Consciousness and the Realization of the "I AM"

Having consciously exited their physical body prior to death; having safely crossed the great abyss; having literally gone "to hell and back"; having journeyed to the very edge of the solar system (to "world's end"); and having travelled back in time to the very inception of life and the cosmos, the more-experienced and better-prepared non-initiate has consequently acquired a much deeper sense of their own immortality. In faithfully following Christ across the threshold, therefore, encountering Christ as the Solar-Christos in the upper-heavenly realm of the sun is the culmination, the transcendent climax to this spiritual journey.

As with Jesus at his baptism in the Jordan, the receptive soul of the non-initiate is now better prepared for a deeper infusion of Christ-consciousness from the Solar-Christos. This higher degree of consciousness from Christ raises up the non-initiate's inner awareness to the reality of their own divinity—their true God-self. The non-initiate realizes with spiritual certainty that their true self, their "I," is a spark of divine reality—the I "IS" eternally real; and therefore God does exist! The non-initiate can knowingly declare "I AM"; and like Jesus himself first realized and proclaimed for all humanity—"I AM one with God"; "I AM a son (a child) of God," created in his image and likeness (Gen 1:26).

7.4 The Realization that God is Love

Once the non-initiate has been temporarily infused with the elevated consciousness of Christ, and has thereby experienced the glorious reality of their own divine-I—their individualized God-self—then an additional, equally-profound revelation is wondrously possible.

Throughout the centuries, theologians, philosophers, mystics and religious believers have all attempted to answer the seemingly-impossible question: "Is there a God?"; that is, "Does God exist?" Together with this age-old perplexity is the equally-imposing question: "If God exists, what is his divine nature—what *is* God?"

At a particularly-luminous stage in following Christ across the threshold—in the glorious realm of the supersensible sun—the faithful non-initiate is more deeply suffused with Christ consciousness; and experientially realizes that God exists, that God IS. The seemingly-impossible question of the ages is triumphantly answered. Furthermore, once the self-realized non-initiate is able to knowingly declare: "I AM; therefore God is"; then they will also transcendently realize: "I AM love; therefore God is love."

It is truly a wondrously-celebratory "revelation from on high," a beatific realization, to experientially know with absolute divine-certainty that one's highest ego-self—one's true I—is a reflection of God. And what an equally-joyous realization to proclaim for all eternity is the divine knowledge that one's true nature is love, because God's divine nature is love.

What could possibly be more jubilant for a sincerely-seeking soul than to know with spiritual certainty that the entire cosmos, including human life, is created out of divine love; that God's love pervades all things from atoms to galaxies.

7.5 Temporarily Becoming One with the Mystic Star

At the very start of the spiritual journey to follow Christ across the threshold, the clairvoyant perception of the nascent non-initiate is temporarily raised to a higher level of observation by a partial infusion of Christ-consciousness.

Thereby, the non-initiate is able to perceive the radiant seed-point of their highest spirit-consciousness that is supersensibly centred in the cerebral area of the pineal gland. In addition, the non-initiate is able to perceive the serene, all-knowing voice of their higher, Christ-infused self; wisely instructing them on how to properly exit the physical body in order to safely and successfully cross the threshold into the spiritual world.

Throughout the harrowing journey, the wise non-initiate continues to listen to the spirit-voice of their higher Christ-self; and to follow the guiding light of the mystic star that continues to appear ahead of their steadfast progression into the unknown. On the return journey to earth, however, during the brief sojourn in the golden realm of the sun, the non-initiate is further infused with the supernal consciousness of Christ-in-the-sun; that is—the exalted Solar-Christos.

With the increased infusion of cosmic Christ-consciousness, for a brief but glorious moment in time, the non-initiate no longer *follows* in the direction of the external point of divine-light; but instead becomes mystically *united* with their highest spirit-self. With the transcendent realization that "I AM one with God," the non-initiate momentarily *becomes* the mystic star of their radiant God-self.

Moreover, instead of *listening* to the external voice of their higher Christed-self, the non-initiate wondrously *becomes* the voice of their Christ-infused God-self for a brief moment in time. And during that time, the non-initiate knows that their undeveloped soul can only bear the powerful, high-vibratory consciousness of the Solar-Christos for a short period of time; and must therefore return to their former level of consciousness soon afterward.

7.6 The "Bodhisattva Vow" and Returning to Earth

During the resplendent—but all-too-brief—period when the non-initiate mystically unites and becomes one with their higher God-self, they supersensibly understand that their undeveloped soul is not capable of extendedly bearing the shattering power of elevated Christ-consciousness without undertaking future initiatory training. Nevertheless, the residual impact of this hallowed experience will transform their entire lives from then on.

Having ascended to the divine summit of human attainment, the spiritually-awakened non-initiate realizes that their God-self transcends all physical barriers and conditions on earth. They can knowingly declare: "In my spirit, I AM free." Moreover, with infused Christ-consciousness they can also triumphantly declare—as was first declared by our saviour, Christ-Jesus: "In my spirit, I AM forever free from the power of death."

With this newly-awakened sense of spiritual freedom acquired while abiding within the supersensible sphere of the sun, the non-initiate realizes that they are also free to return to earth existence, or not. They can freely choose to not return to their vacated physical body; but instead continue to remain in the superphysical world.

However, with their own awareness still upraised with the elevating Christ-consciousness of the Solar-Christos, the awakened non-initiate spiritually intuits that the truly-compassionate, divinely-inspired course of action is to return to physical earth-existence. It is morally understood that the return to earth is not only for the sake of their own continued development; but more importantly, to assist their fellow human beings (and all life on earth) to awaken their own higher God-selves.

Within the esoteric orders of East and West, the self-sacrificial decision to remain on earth for the compassionate sake of others (and not for oneself); instead of continuing to exist in the spiritual world, is known as the "Bodhisattva

Vow."[26] By doing so, the non-initiate voluntarily renounces the self-centred desire to discontinue physical existence, to ignore the suffering of others, and to be exclusively concerned with their own personal happiness.[27]

.

LESSON 8:

RE-AWAKENING FROM THE JOURNEY AND BEING BORN AGAIN

8.1 Experiencing the Two-Fold Nature of Infinity

ONCE THE NON-INITIATE freely decides to leave the realm of the sun; and to return to their somnolent physical body and to life on earth once again, then a feeling of gradual descent immediately begins. As the non-initiate slowly descends through the planetary spheres of Mercury, Venus and the moon, they experience the unusual sensation of somehow shrinking in size; of becoming smaller and smaller as they approach home on earth.

What is likely unbeknownst to the puzzled non-initiate is the esoteric fact that the expansive cosmic-awareness which resulted from the soul-infused Christ-consciousness now begins to slowly withdraw. Shortly before, when the non-initiate was exhilaratingly soaring outwardly in planetary space, their Christed-consciousness was also expanding outwardly in scope and comprehension. Consequently, the expanded awareness which had embraced the entire solar system just a short while before, begins to shrink back to limited, physical sense-awareness once more.

With the cosmic-consciousness of the Solar-Christos in the realm of the sun, the illumined non-initiate experiences something of the infinite greatness and magnitude of God. But when Christ-consciousness begins to diminish as the earth sphere is re-approached from the supersensible sun, the non-initiate's divine self-awareness—their "I AM"—also begins to contract toward the centre of their being.

As awareness of their divine-self becomes increasingly one-pointed and centrally focused, the non-initiate comes to realize first-hand that the infinity of God is two-fold: God is both infinitely great and powerful; as well as infinitely small and humble. In actuality, then, not only does God contain the entire universe within his expansive infinity; but he is also the infinitely-smallest point of reality within the entire universe.

8.2 Experiencing Oneself as a Microcosm of the Macrocosm

If the non-initiate has some prior familiarity with the esoteric doctrine of repeated earth-lives, then the supersensible process of returning to earth and re-joining their physical body is quite similar to the incarnational process of being re-born into a new earth-life. Both cases involve a contraction of cosmic-consciousness prior to physical incarnation. While sojourning in the spiritual world, the consciousness of the discarnate soul temporarily embraces the entire cosmos; or expressed another way, the entire cosmos is temporarily *within* the expanded consciousness of the discarnate soul.

Quite literally, then, every human incarnation on earth involves a psychic contraction of galactic proportions—from a macrocosmic level of superphysical existence in the starry heavens, down to a microcosmic level of physical existence on earth.

8.3   The Iridescent Realm of Imagination

Unlike the ordinary waking experience from deep sleep, when the non-initiate is re-uniting with the somnolent physical and etheric bodies after following Christ across the threshold, they are still consciously aware, and still retain some residual clairvoyance. As a result, instead of becoming immersed in haphazard dream images when entering the etheric body, the awakening non-initiate enters a shimmering, prismatic, etheric realm of multi-coloured, iridescent beauty.

Where normally dream imagery arises spontaneously and uncontrollably, the soon-to-awaken non-initiate quickly discovers that this luminously-pliable etheric material can be consciously and purposefully shaped and molded at will. For a brief period of time before re-entering the vacated physical body, the still-clairvoyant non-initiate is playfully immersed in the etheric "realm of imagination."

8.4   Re-Awakening as a New Person in Christ

Upon awakening in the physical body, the non-initiate triumphantly knows that they arise as a new person in Christ; that in a very real, spiritual sense they have overcome death, and have been "born again." Their "old self" is gone forever. Unlike regular sleep, since the non-initiate is fully aware and partially clairvoyant during the journey with Christ across the threshold, there is a clear memory-record of the supersensible events that occurred.

Thanks to previously-infused Christ-consciousness in the realm of the sun, the awakened non-initiate knows with divine certainty that God exists; and that the divine nature is love. Moreover, they know that their true-self is real and everlasting, a divine-spark from the eternal flame of God. Hereafter, the non-initiate can declare with spiritual authority and power: "I AM one with God, a child of the Almighty, in spiritual union with Christ-Jesus." Truly, they have become an entirely new person through Christ. As biblically expressed by St. Paul:

> Put off your old nature which belongs to your former manner of life ... and be renewed in the spirit of your minds, and put on the new nature, created after the likeness of God in true righteousness and holiness. (Eph 4: 22–24)

> If then you have been raised with Christ, seek the things that are above, where Christ is, seated at the right hand of God. Set your minds on things that are above, not on things that are on earth. For you have died, and your life is hid with Christ in God ... seeing that you have put off the old nature with its practices and have put on the new nature, which is being renewed in knowledge after the image of its creator. (Col 3: 1–3, 9, 10)

Since the non-initiate is detached from their physical senses while sojourning in the spiritual world, they would be unaware of how perilously close the physical body was to death during their absence. In fact, because the physical body is temporarily plunged into such a deep catatonic condition during the out-of-body journey, the non-initiate may discover when they awaken that at some point there has been a loss of bladder control (as typically occurs in death or in a full-faint).

Furthermore, in the realm of the sun when the non-initiate had to freely choose to return to physical earth-existence or not, there was only the thinnest thread of astral contact keeping the physical body alive. If the non-initiate had chosen not to return to earth-life, then the physical body would have peacefully passed away (to the complete mystery of anyone finding the body).

8.5 Radiating Spiritual Light and Attracting the Powers of Darkness

Without esoteric knowledge and initiatory training, the non-initiate is unlikely to notice or understand the profound intrapsychic changes that have resulted from their journey across the threshold. Referring to Figure 1 on page 9, the vast majority of human beings today, function at the level of the sentient soul; while the educated minority function at the level of the intellectual soul. Only a select few have begun to function at the level of the consciousness soul.

With the realization that "I AM one with God; and therefore, I AM a spirit-being," the enlightened non-initiate begins to function at the elevated level of spirit-self. As a result, they begin to increasingly radiate an aureole of supersensible light from the third-eye centre in the head. Even though the non-initiate may not be able to clairvoyantly perceive this luminous change, it is noticeably visible to a variety of superphysical beings (such as angels and archangels).

Unfortunately, this newly-ignited spiritual light is perceived as a painful threat to a far-different host of superphysical beings that are inimical to human life (such as ahrimanic and luciferic beings). Consequently, it's crucially important for the spiritually-awakened non-initiate to be psychically prepared for periodic mental and emotional assaults by the spirits of darkness.

Nevertheless, the non-initiate's newly-acquired spiritual consciousness also unites them with powerful, benevolent superphysical beings that will guide and protect them during times of spiritual crisis. In any event, the spiritual consciousness that was acquired by following Christ across the threshold into the spiritual world will continue to transform and elevate the Christed non-initiate for the rest of their earthly life and beyond.

LESSON 9:

THE AFTER-DEATH JOURNEY OF CHRIST-JESUS AS THE TEMPLATE FOR COSMIC RE-CREATION

9.1 Christ's Descent into Hell to Free the Captive Souls

EVEN THOUGH THE NON-INITIATE is unlikely to know at the time, their own Christ-infused journey across the threshold is actually a diminished and abbreviated replication of Christ's own world-altering, after-death journey. In following Christ across the threshold, then, the non-initiate is unknowingly repeating the same journey that Christ-Jesus undertook after his crucifixion.

Unfortunately, conventional Christianity has very little insight regarding the post-mortem existence of Christ-Jesus between the crucifixion and the resurrection. Nevertheless, it is traditionally accepted that our Saviour experienced the full pangs of physical death, in that there was an actual separation of his soul from his body. The question is, then: "Did Christ's soul remain with his body in the tomb until his resurrection, or did it temporarily descend into hell."

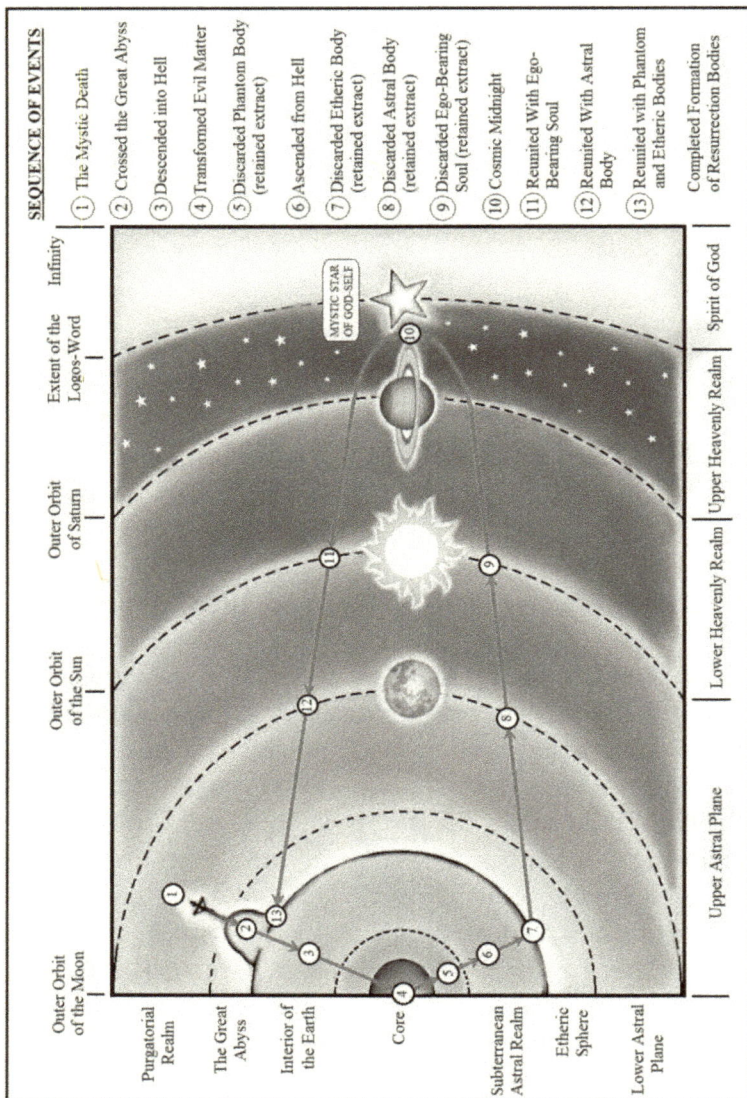

SEQUENCE OF EVENTS

1. The Mystic Death
2. Crossed the Great Abyss
3. Descended into Hell
4. Transformed Evil Matter
5. Discarded Phantom Body (retained extract)
6. Ascended from Hell
7. Discarded Etheric Body (retained extract)
8. Discarded Astral Body (retained extract)
9. Discarded Ego-Bearing Soul (retained extract)
10. Cosmic Midnight
11. Reunited With Ego-Bearing Soul
12. Reunited With Astral Body
13. Reunited with Phantom and Etheric Bodies
    Completed Formation of Resurrection Bodies

Figure 6: The After-Death Journey of Christ-Jesus

64

Most Protestant denominations tend to believe that Christ's soul did not descend into hell; but that the painful agonies of hell were experienced on the cross prior to death. The Catholic, Greek Orthodox and Lutheran denominations, however, believe in a literal descent into hell by Christ-Jesus; although they differ as to the reasons why. The Lutheran belief is that Christ journeyed to hell in order to proclaim victory over the devil and all the powers of darkness. The Catholic and Orthodox belief is that our Saviour primarily descended into hell in order to release the righteous souls held captive there since the fall from paradise; as well as to proclaim victory over hell and the devil. As explained in the *Catechism of the Catholic Church*:

> The frequent New Testament affirmations that Jesus was "raised from the dead" presuppose that the crucified one sojourned in the realm of the dead prior to his resurrection. This was the first meaning given in the apostolic preaching to Christ's descent into hell: that Jesus, like all men, experienced death and in his soul joined the others in the realm of the dead. But he descended there as Saviour, proclaiming the Good News to the spirits imprisoned there. (Paragraph 632)

> Scripture calls the abode of the dead, to which the dead Christ went down, "hell"—Sheol in Hebrew or Hades in Greek—because those who are there are deprived of the vision of God ... "It is precisely these holy souls, who awaited their Saviour in Abraham's bosom, whom Christ the Lord delivered when he descended into hell." Jesus did not descend into hell to deliver the damned, nor to destroy the hell of damnation, but to free the just who had gone before him. (Paragraph 633)

> "The gospel was preached even to the dead." The descent into hell brings the Gospel message of salvation to complete fulfillment. This is the last phase of Jesus'

messianic mission, a phase which is condensed in time but vast in its real significance: the spread of Christ's redemptive work to all men of all times and all places, for all who are saved have been made sharers in the redemption. (Paragraph 634)

Jesus, "the Author of life," by dying destroyed "him who has the power of death, that is, the devil, and [delivered] all those who through fear of death were subject to lifelong bondage." Henceforth the risen Christ holds "the keys of Death and Hades," so that "at the name of Jesus every knee should bow, in heaven and on earth and under the earth." (Paragraph 635)

Fortunately, esoteric-Christianity is able to provide much more detailed and comprehensive information about Christ-Jesus' after-death existence prior to his resurrection.[28] For instance, it is a supersensible fact that Christ-Jesus did indeed cross the great abyss and descend into the subterranean underworld immediately after death. Although his mineral, corporeal body was left behind in the tomb, our Saviour still retained the etheric, astral, soul and spiritual vehicles which continued to be permeated by the forces of the exalted Solar-Christos.

Unlike the out-of-body non-initiate who is only temporarily infused with the consciousness of the Solar-Christos in the realm of the sun, Jesus was (and is) more deeply and enduringly permeated by the presence of the Solar-Christos—even when he was physically active on earth! Consequently, when the discarnate Christ-Jesus descended into the dark underworld, this ingress acted as a powerful shaft of spiritual lightning that penetrated to the very core of the planet.

As a result, the omnipotent light of divine love began to immediately transform and transmute the entire debased interior of planet earth. This included not only the degenerate matter and energy contained within the earth; but since Christ-Jesus was supernally clairvoyant, he was able to perceive and to overcome the powerfully-evil beings—such as Ahriman and Sorath—who dwelt within the earth as well. Consequently, the penetrating shaft of Christ-light provided the first ray of heavenly hope for righteous souls trapped in subterranean darkness after death.

9.2 Transmuting the Debased Primordial Matter and Energy at the Earth's Core

When the Christ-infused non-initiate descends into the subterranean underworld, they imitate Christ-Jesus by also bringing spiritual light into the earth's interior. Of course, the degree of spiritual light brought by the non-initiate is modest in comparison to the superplanetary brilliance of the Solar-Christos radiating from Christ-Jesus. Nevertheless, even a small amount of spiritual light contributes to the long-term transformation of the earth; and positively assists our Saviour in establishing a "new heaven and a new earth" (Rev 21:1).

Physically establishing a new heaven (cosmos) and a new earth; that is—spiritually transmuting and transforming universal matter and energy—first began when Christ-Jesus penetrated to the very centre of the earth. By infusing divine love into the evilly-corrupted primeval material at the earth's core, our Saviour miraculously turned it "inside out." Where before this debased matter and energy was relentlessly pulling everything around it in a backward, retrograde direction that was opposed to divine progress, with Christ's spiritual reversal this matter and energy is now slowly evolving in a positive, divine direction.

Due to Christ's descent into hell, then, divine love has become an uplifting, elevating force within universal matter and energy, that will eventually transform the entire cosmos.[29]

What the non-initiate experiences as a horrible retching and regurgitation of convulsing and writhing substance at the earth's core is in fact the material inversion of the cosmos first generated by the divine love indwelling Christ-Jesus. Once again, by imitating the after-death journey of our Saviour, the non-initiate also contributes in a small but important way to the spiritualization of degenerate matter and energy at the earth's core.

As discussed in sub-chapter 4.6 on page 36, penetrating deeper into the earth's interior is simultaneously a journey back in time, to the very inception of our present-day universe. Consequently, when Christ-Jesus reversed the backward, retrograde pull of atavistic matter and energy comprising the earth's interior, he also everted the corrupted, counter-evolutionary time-travel that contracted back toward a falsely-distorted cosmic genesis.

Over vast stretches of time, Sorath the sun-demon has been corrupting atavistic primordial matter and energy in a megalomaniacal attempt to replace the true, divinely-generated universe with his own nefariously-willed conception. By transmuting Sorath's debased matter and energy, Christ-Jesus activated the gradual displacement of the sun-demon's pseudo-universe.

By following Christ into the infernal underworld, the non-initiate also unknowingly contributes in a small but significant way to the dissipation of Sorath's evil goal of replacing our God-directed cosmos with his own demon-directed aberration.

9.3 Overcoming Bodily Densification and Uniting with God the Son

By planting the spiritual spark of divine love in the heart of darkness at the earth's core, Christ-Jesus overcame the densifying material consequences of "original sin"; that is, he arrested and reverted the sorathic tendency of the physical human body to become increasingly denser and more chemically crystallized as a result of luciferic and ahrimanic interference in the primordial past.[30]

Likewise for the non-initiate, by following Christ into hell and then rising above it, the infernal gravitational grip of debased, sorathic matter and energy on their own elemental physical body is finally broken. As a result, the physical body of the non-initiate will gradually become more tenuous, ephemeral and angelically refined throughout all future re-embodiments.

When Christ-Jesus penetrated the infernal centre of the earth after death, the superplanetary forces of the Solar-Christos planted a spark of spiritual light into the heart of planetary darkness. Over time, this spark will increasingly grow and expand; eventually re-uniting the earth with the sun. Thereafter, the earth will be transformed into a miniature sun within the solar embrace of the greater sun-sphere.

After planting the radiant seed of solar renewal within the core of the earth, Christ-Jesus rose victoriously from the transmuted and transformed underworld. In his upward ascension from hell, our Saviour proceeded to discard his various lower vehicles of consciousness in rapid succession. This process entirely conforms with what typically occurs to every human being after death. In order to ascend to higher and higher levels of existence in the spiritual world, one must discard the lower vehicles of consciousness that "weigh" the spirit down.

Not surprisingly, the spiritually-charged events of our Saviour's after-death journey were highly accelerated. While the process of discarding the physical body, etheric body, astral body and soul vehicles typical takes decades, years and centuries to accomplish, with Christ-Jesus this was easily done in a matter of hours and days.

In the case of the non-initiate rising upwardly from hell and soaring outwardly into planetary space, there was no similar discarding of body and soul vehicles because the non-initiate is not dead and remains vitally connected to these vehicles. In addition, when Christ-Jesus soared victoriously through planetary space he was fully clairvoyant of the various planetary spheres and of the superphysical beings associated with them.

Even more significantly, upon reaching the outer sphere of Saturn, our Saviour was not hurled back to the earth as happens with the non-initiate; but instead, he continued to expand farther and farther into cosmic space in the direction of his own mystic God-star. After death, travelling past the "switching station" of Saturn typically occurs; but not if the soul-traveler is still alive, as is the case with a non-initiate. Even so, to everyone after death there comes a point long before the outer edge of the cosmos is reached, when the soul in heaven is irresistibly drawn back toward a new birth on earth. In esoteric science, the point at which this occurs is known as "cosmic midnight" (or "the great midnight-hour of existence").

In the unique case of Christ-Jesus, however, our Saviour continued to ascend through the highest heavenly-realms of the cherubim and seraphim in the direction of his own mystic God-star. It was only after reaching the most spiritualized level of the cosmos that our Saviour's after-death ascension came to rest. It was at this empyrean point of creation that Christ-Jesus was able to spiritually unite with God the Son; and could truthfully declare: "I AM one with God, the son of the Almighty Father."

Having wondrously achieved spiritual union with God, Christ-Jesus could hereafter assist struggling humanity to similarly unite with God. To do that, however, he would have to return to earth. As was similarly replicated by the non-initiate in the realm of the sun, Christ-Jesus was entirely free to return to earth, or to continue remaining in the spiritual world. Once again, as morally replicated by the non-initiate, Christ-Jesus unquestioningly knew that the self-sacrificing nature of divine love is to help those in need; so of course he freely chose to return to earth. Whereas the non-initiate wisely chooses to take the "Bodhisattva Vow," Christ-Jesus took the exalted "Vow of World Saviour"; that is, the pledge before God to compassionately assist struggling humanity until "the end of the age" (Matt 28:20).

9.4 Re-Uniting and Resurrecting the Redeemed Body and Soul Vehicles

When the typical soul returns to earthly re-embodiment from the heavenly realms, as they gradually descend through the various planetary spheres, new etheric, astral and soul vehicles are fashioned that will unite with the physical body provided by the parents. The vehicles from their previous incarnation, having been successively discarded after death, gradually disintegrated into their cosmic components.

In the unique case of Christ-Jesus, however, even though he rapidly discarded his body and soul vehicles after death, they remained entirely perfect and complete due to the purifying, redemptive power of the Solar-Christos.[31] As a result, our Saviour did not need to fashion new body and soul vehicles on returning to earth; he simply re-united with his perfectly-preserved discarded ones. Furthermore, there was no need for Christ-Jesus to unite with a different, parentally-provided physical body, since his previous physical phantom was also perfectly preserved and free from dense chemical attraction.

When Christ-Jesus re-united with his previous body and soul vehicles, this was not simply a replication of his previous existence. Since he had united his highest-self with God the

Son at cosmic midnight and assumed the responsibility of World Saviour, Christ-Jesus was able to further infuse his previous vehicles with the increased power of divine love. This of course entirely transformed his "redeemed" body and soul vehicles into more-advanced, "resurrected" body and soul vehicles.

After re-uniting and resurrecting his physical phantom, our Saviour gloriously and triumphantly arose from the tomb, and began his lofty mission as World Saviour. In his divinely-infused resurrected form, Christ-Jesus has the power to physically appear and disappear at will. He can intangibly pass through solid walls, or tangibly consume solid food if need be. In other words, in his divinely-resurrected form, Christ-Jesus can now pass from heaven to earth at will.

When the non-initiate gloriously awakens from the spiritual journey with Christ across the threshold, they moderately mirror our Saviour's triumphant resurrection from the tomb. In both cases the sting of death has been overcome by a spiritual union with God. With the non-initiate, however, the infusion of Christ-consciousness that enabled this divine oneness to occur was only temporary; whereas with Christ-Jesus, the intrapsychic penetration and permeation of the Solar-Christos is much deeper and more permanent.

9.5 Becoming the New Regent of the Earth

When Christ-Jesus accepted his sacred mission as World Saviour, he also assumed the associated responsibility of "Planetary Regent"; that is, the added function of "Spirit of the Earth." As such, the entire evolution of the earth is now under his divinely-appointed leadership.

In this immense capacity, Christ-Jesus replicates his after-death journey on a planetary level with the seasonal "inbreathing" and "outbreathing" rhythm of the earth. During the winter months (which differ in each hemisphere), the new Regent of the Earth descends to the heart of the planetary to reinforce and advance his transformative spiritualization of subterranean evil. During the summer months, Christ-Jesus as Planetary Regent, re-ascends to the empyrean edge of the cosmos to re-strengthen and expand his spiritual union with God.

Since world evolution proceeds at an exceedingly gradual and incremental pace, it is crucially necessary for Christ-Jesus to planetarily descend and cosmically reascend each season in order to spiritually upraise the planet into the future "new earth." Moreover, even though the contribution is much more modest, every time a non-initiate follows Christ across the threshold, this helps our Saviour to spiritually transform the earth, and to advance struggling humanity.

LESSON 10:

CONCLUSION

10.1 Transforming the Earth's Interior Through Mystic-Christian Initiation

EVEN THOUGH THESE LESSONS are intended to be an esoteric guide for the non-initiate, it is also valuable to understand the significant contributions being made to world transformation through Christian initiation. Furthermore, after the non-initiate has experienced the life-altering experience of following Christ across the threshold, they may very well decide to pursue a path of initiation to further their esoteric development.

If the non-initiate has journeyed into the subterranean underworld, they will have some basic clairvoyant experience of the various infernal levels (or layers). It is therefore of esoteric interest to note that the seven developmental stages of Mystic-Christian initiation will unfold and expand the clairvoyant ability to perceive and transform the superphysical layers of the earth's interior.

Without going into unnecessary detail, as understood in

spiritual science there are seven stages of Mystic-Christian initiation:

1. the Washing of the Feet
2. the Scourging
3. the Crowning with Thorns
4. the Carrying of the Cross
5. the Mystic Death
6. the Entombment (or Burial)
7. the Resurrection

As each stage is mystically experienced by the Christian initiate, a corresponding layer within the subterranean earth becomes clairvoyantly perceptible. As described by Rudolf Steiner in a lecture presented on 16 April 1906, entitled: "The Interior of the Earth and Volcanic Eruptions":

> Something truly remarkable emerges from each stage of [Mystic-Christian] initiation in relation to the scientific investigation of the earth. A further, deeper layer of our earth becomes transparent at each stage. Whoever has reached the first stage of initiation can penetrate the first layer of the earth. Whoever has reached the second stage penetrates to the second layer, which looks very different. One who has borne the Crown of Thorns sees the third layer. Then comes the stage of Cross-Bearing, when the fourth layer becomes visible. The fifth stage, Mystic Death, opens up a further layer. There follows the sixth stage, that of Entombment. The seventh layer corresponds to the Resurrection. Thus there are seven consecutive layers. Beyond these seven, which are the levels a person reaches in going through these seven stages of initiation, lie two more layers—an eighth and a ninth layer. The inner earth therefore consists of nine layers.

Not only do the subterranean layers become clairvoyantly

visible to the Mystic-Christian initiate, but since each stage of initiation brings them into closer union with Christ-Jesus, the initiate acquires greater and greater capacity to help spiritualize the earth's interior through divine love.

10.2 The Secret Process of Cosmic Evolution

In order to better understand the process of crossing the threshold during sleep and after death, it is necessary to explain certain universal laws that apply throughout the cosmos. For example, in order to better understand why the discarnate soul (in sleep or in death) descends to the centre of the earth before ascending into planetary space, it is necessary to know more about the "universal law of vibratory rhythm." Likewise, in order to better understand why the unbounded soul in heaven is reborn into a confined body on earth, it is also necessary to know about the "universal law of recapitulation."

To begin with, it is encouraging to note that today both physical science and esoteric science agree that our expanding universe had a "point" of origin in the primeval past. Nevertheless, the physical science of cosmogony contends that the universe began about 13.7 billion years ago as an infinitely-small, infinitely hot, and infinitely dense point of origin termed a "singularity." Within this singularity was contained all universal matter, energy, space and time.

Esoteric science, on the other hand, asserts that the universe began as a tiny "seed" of cosmic creation conceived vast ages ago within the infinite and eternal mind of God. Within the divine point of universal genesis was contained all potential matter, energy, space and time—as well as consciousness (mind) and life. Remarkably, Georges Lemaître (1894–1966), the Catholic priest, astronomer and physicist who first mathematically postulated an expanding universe from a primordial beginning (later known as the "Big Bang"), perceptively termed the point of origin, the "Primal Atom" or the "Cosmic Egg."

To esoteric understanding, then, all life in the universe began as a divinely-conceived cosmic seed (or egg). This explains why, even today, all life on earth springs from a seed or egg.[32] Life does not spontaneously generate from inanimate matter ("abiogenesis"). The observable fact that only life can reproduce life—that a new life-form can only proceed from an egg or seed produced by another life-form—was succinctly expressed by English physician William Harvey (1578–1657) with the famous Latin phrase: *"Omne vivum ex ovo"* ("All life comes from an egg").

Predictably, as the infinitesimal seed of cosmic creation first began to grow and expand, structural formation was extremely primitive and initial progress was excruciatingly slow. One noticeable characteristic of cosmic expansion was an inherent propensity (or universal law) to formulate and to replicate germinal centres of activity. Over vast stretches of time, these elementary centres of activity gradually developed into rudimentary subatomic particles, then into basic atomic particles, then into simple molecules, and eventually into stars and galaxies.

Since life and consciousness were also contained within the divine seed of cosmic creation, elementary life-forms also began to slowly develop as the cosmos continued to expand in time and space. As with universal matter and energy, life-forms also conformed to the intrinsic universal compulsion to formulate individual centres of activity, and then to replicate them. Moreover, as with the development of matter and energy, life-forms slowly progressed from rudimentary to complex over vast periods of cosmic time.

Elementary life-forms that arose at the beginning of time were exceedingly tenuous and diaphanous, being formulated out of etheric and astral substance. Consequently, they would be invisible to physical sight; and would therefore be undetectable and unacknowledged by the physical science of today.

In any event, all life-forms (as well as all matter and energy) were additionally subject to a universal law of vibratory rhythm; that is, everything in the universe fluctuates between periods of contraction and expansion, and between periods of activity and rest. Even the entire universe itself undergoes vast periods of cosmic expansion and cosmic collapse; between vast periods of cosmic activity and cosmic rest. In esoteric fact, our present universe is now expanding from a previous cosmic collapse (which has occurred a number of times during the exceedingly-remote and primeval past.

The alternation between activity and rest is readily observable with the various life-forms existing on earth. For example, plant-life tends to be more active during the sun-lit, daytime hours; and more at rest during the dark, nightime hours. Likewise during the seasons: plant-life growth and activity occurs mostly during the warm summer months; whereas during the cold winter months, plant-life will undergo a period of repose and dormancy.

Not only plant-life, but animal-life and human-life also visibly alternate between activity and rest. The most noticeable and familiar alternation is that between wakeful activity (usually during the day) and restful sleep (usually during the night). As with plant-life, the alternation between activity and rest for animal-life and for human-life is also affected by the cycle of the seasons. Many animals in cold northern climates will restfully hibernate during the winter months, and resume normal activity when spring re-arrives.

Unfortunately with modern-day human-life, particularly in urban settings with artificial light and climate-controlling technology (such as furnace-heaters and air-conditioners), the seasonal rhythms are much easier to ignore. Nevertheless, in more rural settings, human-life still responds to the seasonal alternation between wintery indoor quietude and reflection, and summery outdoor recreation and activity.

In the case of all life-forms on earth, there is also an alternation between physical life and physical death.[33] Physical life is characterized by growth and activity; whereas in death all physical activity observably ceases. Especially in the case of human-life, the alternation between physical life and death is often compared to that of waking and sleeping. Death is popularly described as the "big sleep," and after death one is described as "resting in peace."[35]

In order for life-forms (in general) to continue to exist after death, it is necessary to reproduce; that is, it is necessary to produce another similar life-form. In the case of complex, multi-celled life-forms, such as plants, animals and humans, physical reproduction is accomplished by generating a miniature single-celled genetic "blueprint" of the parent life-form.[34] In this connection, biological science currently contends that all physical life-forms on earth began as a single cell. In other words, the reproductive process of generating a fertilized seed or egg can be seen as an accelerated repetition of the entire evolutionary process of a life-form from the very beginning.

It's a little-acknowledged fact of life that in order to reproduce a new life-form (be it plant, animal or human) it is necessary to restart from the evolutionary beginning as a single cell. In other words, in order to reproduce an existing, complex life-form it is necessary to go back in time and recapitulate the entire evolutionary process up to the present day. Fortunately the recapitulation process is highly accelerated and much more refined than the original evolutionary process.

For example, the developing human child from fertilized ovum to birth, recapitulates in nine months what previously took millions of evolutionary years to accomplish. Moreover, each time a new life-form is reproduced, imperceptively-small improvements are incorporated into the fertilized egg or seed. Thereby, the life-form continues to progressively evolve and advance. Positive improvements are added to the recapitulation process, so that evolutionary progress spirals upward, rather than simply going around and around without any positive development.

From the foregoing information, it will be better understood that in order to begin spiritual life on the other side of the threshold (even temporarily, as in sleep) it is necessary to go back in time to the very inception of human life in the cosmos. Currently, this entails a superphysical descent into the dark subterranean underworld through the anachronistic, residual matter and energy from previous archaic periods of planetary development—first the Ancient Moon Period; then the Ancient Sun Period; and lastly the Ancient Saturn Period.

Together with travelling back in time, the descent into the underworld also entails a supersensible contraction towards the centre of the earth. When human individuals experience an analogous intrapsychic contraction toward the centre of their being, this serves to strengthen separate ego-awareness. When the non-initiate or deceased soul experiences a contraction toward the centre of the earth, then they become increasingly conscious of the planetary-ego (and not their own).

Unfortunately over time, the evil influence of the sun-demon Sorath has corrupted the planetary-ego, resulting in it becoming the subterranean source of black magic on earth. Thankfully, with Christ-Jesus becoming the new regent of the earth, the false ego of the planet is slowly being transformed into the divine ego of our Saviour.

In accordance with the universal law of vibrational rhythm, the centripetal contraction toward the centre of the earth is rhythmically followed by a centrifugal expansion toward the planetary or cosmic periphery. Likewise when the non-initiate or the incarnating soul is returning to earth from the heavenly regions, there is a gradual contraction of expanded cosmic consciousness down to physical-sensory awareness. In the case of a newly-incarnating soul, they begin the contraction process by psychically connecting with the fertilized ovum provided by the future parents. Once the incarnational process is complete, then the soul begins a new physical life of expansion, growth and development, in accordance with the universal law of vibrational rhythm.

10.3 The Restorative Soul-Journey of Sleep

It is rather astounding for the non-initiate to discover that in every instance of deep, prolonged sleep, the soul temporarily leaves the body and crosses the threshold into the spiritual world. Except for esoteric students and initiates, few people today are aware of this fact, particularly since waking consciousness is normally extinguished during sleep. It is only when the non-initiate is karmically infused with Christ-consciousness that the spiritual journey during sleep is clairvoyantly perceived.

From an esoteric understanding, there are a number of very good reasons for the typical lack of consciousness during sleep. For one, unless an individual has developed the necessary superphysical senses, they will not be able to clairvoyantly perceive the environment, events and beings of the spiritual world. For another, unless an individual has positively confronted and overcome the negative influence of their subconsciously-stored past wrongdoings, this accumulated psychic detritus will act as a "guardian of the threshold" to prevent them from crossing over in full-consciousness.

As an additional reason, without adequate esoteric

preparation and knowledgeable guidance (from Christ-Jesus or an initiate-hierophant) the terrifying experiences of consciously crossing the threshold would be seriously soul shattering for most individuals. One final reason for remaining unconscious during sleep is to prevent naïve, foolhardy, inept or malicious individuals harming themselves or others by toying or meddling with powerful life-forces in the spiritual world.[36]

Even though the supersensible journey undertaken during sleep remains unconscious for most individuals today, it is still astonishing to realize that every instance of deep slumber engenders a travel back in time to the primordial beginning of physical-sensory human-life on earth. Equally amazing is the esoteric fact that this time-reversal can occur in a matter of hours, or minutes, or even seconds; since time is much more "fluid" in the supersensible world. This phenomenon was well described by Rudolf Steiner in a lecture given on 16 May 1923, entitled: "On the Nature and Destiny of Man and World" (and published in *Man's Being, His Destiny and World-Evolution*; 1966):

> At the moment of falling asleep, we are transported backward through the whole course of time. We are brought back to *that* moment when we descended from the heavenly realms to earth ... We return, across *time*, to the starting-point of our earth-life. Hence, while the physical and etheric body are lying in bed, the ego and astral body have gone back across time to an earlier moment.
>
> [E]vents that have stretched themselves out over several hours may ... be passed through again almost instantly. The conditions of time change in the sleeping state. Time may be completely compressed.

For the non-initiate who has followed Christ across the threshold into the spiritual world, they can better understand how and why the descent into the underworld and the ascent into the planetary spheres is vitally necessary during sleep. The descent into the earth's interior is intended to restore the physical forces of the body that have been depleted by the damaging activities performed during waking life. Correspondingly, by ascending into planetary space and immersing in a cosmic ocean of life-giving energy, the superphysical forces of the soul and spirit are also restored to vibrant health again.

10.4 Preparation for the Cosmic Journey after Death

Even if for some reason, the non-initiate is unable to follow Christ across the threshold in this life, the lessons contained in this guide will definitely help prepare them for the journey after death. Since all life-forms are subject to the universal law of vibratory rhythm and the universal law of recapitulation, the spiritual journeys during sleep and after death will be similarly experienced by every human being. Of course there will be definite individual differences as well; since every human life is biologically similar, but psychologically unique.

Even though the soul is much more aware of the spiritual world after death, this does not necessarily mean that they will consciously experience all the events of a Christ-infused spiritual journey. For instance, after a few days of reviewing the memory tableau of their previous life on earth, most deceased individuals naturally slip into a deep soul-slumber in which they vividly experience the joy and sorrow that their actions on earth have caused to others. This could be described as the prolonged, after-death equivalent of dream-filled sleep. During this time, most discarnate souls are entirely unaware of passing through the frightening, subterranean underworld.

The period of vividly-experienced soul-slumber (also known as "purgatory" in the West and "kamaloka" in the East), usually lasts for about one-third the length of a person's life. It is only after the discarnate soul has awakened from the prolonged soul-slumber that they become more aware of their supersensible surroundings, and also begin to expand outwardly through the planetary spheres.

Even though the deceased soul, when physically alive, was usually unconscious during sleep due to a lack of initiatory development, after death they gradually become more and more supersensibly aware of their surroundings as they pass through the planetary spheres. This increase in clairvoyant perception is primarily due to the temporary infusion of higher consciousness from their guardian angel and other celestial beings. This celestial infusion is necessary in order for the deceased soul to properly advance in the heavenly realms, and thereby begin to prepare for their subsequent rebirth.

Moreover, if the departed soul has been a dedicated and faithful disciple of Christ-Jesus during their previous lifetime, then our Saviour will additionally raise their supersensible awareness with infused divine-consciousness during the after-death journey. Furthermore, if the departed soul—as a non-initiate—followed Christ across the threshold during life, then they can be assured that our Saviour will additionally guide and re-infuse them with his exalted divine-consciousness after death as well.

ADDENDUM

WHEN AUSTRIAN PHILOSOPHER and eminent esotericist Rudolf Steiner (1861–1925) established the School of Spiritual Science at the Christmas Conference in Dornach, Switzerland in 1923, he envisioned a graded program of three classes—similar to first, second and third-year university courses—but with an esoteric content. Throughout 1924, he was able to formulate nineteen fundamental lessons for the First Class. Unfortunately, due to his untimely death on 30 March 1925, Steiner was unable to formulate the lessons for the Second and Third Classes.

Departing from the intentionally-academic prose style of his spiritual-scientific discourses, Steiner crafted the nineteen lessons of the First Class in the form of poetic-style mantras. This was deliberately done to facilitate a more affective, meditative approach to esoteric development; rather than an intellectual, scholarly approach.

To be consistent with the dispassionate, objective approach of empirical science, Steiner de-emphasized subjective expressions of emotion and sentiment in his spiritual-scientific discourses. Nevertheless, he maintained that the emotional aspect of lofty spiritual ideas would be spontaneously inflamed as a natural by-product of intellectually rigorous spiritual thinking.

Conversely, the intended developmental challenge with the poetic mantras of the nineteen lessons is to meditatively comprehend the emotionally-stimulating visualizations and poetic descriptions in order to express the esoteric content in clear, intellectual concepts. With this particular meditative path of esoteric development, rather than the teacher (Rudolf Steiner) presenting the student with clear, intellectual concepts of the spiritual world in a lecture-style format, students are encouraged to actively generate their own corresponding ideas from the mantric descriptions.

Clearly, as a meditative path to esoteric development, the School of Spiritual Science was not intended by Rudolf Steiner to be a new method of modern initiation. There are no specific exercises or particular practices in the nineteen lessons that are designed to stimulate and unfold the psycho-spiritual centres of clairvoyant perception; or to consciously detach the soul vehicles from the physical body.

What is intended is for the student of the School to gain an intellectual familiarity and an emotional connection to the spiritual world, together with its beings and events—such as the guardian of the threshold, the abyss and crossing the threshold; and to gain an understanding of the complex interactions amongst the various levels of the celestial hierarchy.

Obviously there was no need for an additional path of modern initiation, since Rudolf Steiner made it abundantly clear in his discourses that there already exist two safe and effective paths of initiation specifically designed for modern-day spiritual development. The Mystic-Christian path of initiation that uses the Gospel of John as its guidebook has been successfully applied for centuries, particularly within the various monastic orders. Additionally, the Rosicrucian-Christian path of initiation that was established in the fifteenth century by Christian Rosenkreutz is specifically designed for those who are unable to lead a more cloistered, reclusive lifestyle.[37]

To re-state, then, the School of Spiritual Science, as exemplified by the nineteen lessons of the First Class, is a meditative (not initiatory) path of esoteric development that is intended to emotionally and intellectually prepare students for conscious life in the spiritual world. Therefore, even though Rudolf Steiner was unable to formulate the Second and Third Classes, it is reasonable to conclude that these more advanced classes would have continued and further deepened the emotional and intellectual preparation needed for successful life in the spiritual world.

It also seems reasonable to conclude (though some anthroposophists are likely to challenge this) that the responsibility to complete a Second and a Third Class for the School of Spiritual Science falls on the anthroposophical community that continues Rudolf Steiner's legacy of esoteric work in the world. Some present-day anthroposophists will predictably object on the grounds that there is no anthroposophist living now (or in the past) who is equal to Rudolf Steiner in initiatory development and achievement. Therefore, no one is sufficiently qualified to continue and extend his illustrious work.

While it is certainly true that Rudolf Steiner is one of the most highly-advanced initiates to historically appear on the world stage, it is also true that he has always expected his anthroposophical followers to build-on, expand and advance the esoteric work that he began—to the best of their limited abilities. Otherwise, the transformative spiritual downpouring that he inaugurated will quickly stagnate, ossify and cease to advance.

This is somewhat analogous to Christ-Jesus and his own less-advanced followers. If no one bothered to follow in the Master's footsteps because of his exalted divine nature, then his transformative mission on earth would cease to progressively move forward. Our Saviour likewise expects his followers to continue his work on earth to the best of their limited abilities.

It is my heartfelt and humble contention, therefore, that since the ten lessons contained here, in *Following Christ Across the Threshold: The Non-Initiate's Guide to Entering the Spiritual World*, are also a meditative path to esoteric development, they can well be used as a basis for the Second Class of the School of Spiritual Science. While these particular lessons are not in the mantra-style of the nineteen lessons, I don't believe this is exclusively necessary; as long as they continue to advance the emotional and intellectual preparation needed to confidently enter the spiritual world in a safe and Christ-directed way.

While it is expected that the leadership of the General Anthroposophical Society will be reluctant at the present time to formally adopt these ten lessons as a basis for the unrealized Second Class; nevertheless, individual students of the School of Spiritual Science are certainly free to informally use them to enhance the nineteen lessons of the First Class. I am more than confident that those students who decide to consider and meditate on these deeply-esoteric lessons will be brought closer to Christ-Jesus, to God and to their higher spirit-selves—which would undoubtedly meet with the approval of Rudolf Steiner and St. Michael the Archai (who spiritually sponsors the School).

NOTES

INTRODUCTION

1. Regarding the biblical figure of St. John, many modern scholars acknowledge that there existed two concurrent Johns: (1) John the apostle, who was the son of Zebedee and the brother of James the ("greater") apostle; and (2) John the evangelist, who was the author of the Gospel of John, the two Letters of John and the Book of Revelation.

    According to esoteric Christianity, John the evangelist—"the disciple whom Jesus loved"—is understood to be the same person known biblically as Lazarus. After being "raised from the dead" in an openly-displayed mystic-initiation, Lazarus thereafter assumed the "re-born name" of John.

2. The Church of St. Peter is here understood to include both Catholic and Eastern Orthodox Christianity; since there was only "one, holy, catholic (universal) and apostolic" Christian Church in the first centuries after Christ. It was only after the Great Schism of 1054 that they have become two separate halves of the same, original Petrine Church.

3. The authentic Rosicrucian Order is a highly-secretive, esoteric-Christian fraternity that was established during the thirteenth century by Christian Rosenkreutz, an incarnation of St. John the evangelist. While Rosicrucian initiates have quietly and anonymously contributed in numerous ways to human and social advancement over the centuries, the organization itself remains securely concealed from public view to this very day.

   From the very beginning, this policy of strict secrecy was never due to elitism, chauvinism or for covert power and control; but rather for protection from psychic attack, religious persecution and undue public attention. Throughout history there have been a great many spurious public organizations all falsely claiming to be the one, true Rosicrucian Order.

   In the late-nineteenth and early-twentieth century, a substantial outpouring of Rosicrucian knowledge and teaching was made publicly available by the highly-advanced initiate, Rudolf Steiner (1861–1925), the founder of anthroposophy.

4. The classic guide to the Rosicrucian-Christian path of initiation was originally written in German, and publicized for the first time by Rudolf Steiner in 1904. Because of different English translations, the book is known by various titles; such as: *Knowledge of the Higher Worlds and its Attainment* (1986); *How to Know Higher Worlds: A Modern Path of Initiation* (1994); *Knowledge of the Higher Worlds: How is it Achieved?* (2009).

5. Karma is here understood as the "universal law of spiritual cause and effect." Similar to the physical world where a physical action will produce a corresponding physical effect; in the superphysical world, thoughts, feelings and actions will also have corresponding effects that will shape, influence, impact and determine the conditions and attributes of subsequent incarnations.

LESSON 1

6. For the highly-trained initiate with developed supersensible perception (such as Rudolf Steiner), the lesser guardian of the threshold appears as a threefold spectral apparition. The karmic corruption of soul-willing appears as a spectral beast with a parched form, crooked back, bony head and dull, blunt-blue skin that arouses fear of the spiritual world. The karmic corruption of soul-feeling appears as a spectral beast with a loathsome shape of yellow and spotted-grey skin, and a distorted, scornful countenance with bared teeth that arouses hatred of the spiritual world. The karmic corruption of soul-thinking appears as a dirty-red, slouching spectral beast with a glassy eye and a long split-mouth that arouses doubt about the spiritual world.

7. As one example, in this author's own experience, what unexpectedly appeared in his twenty-first year was a gigantic, hideously-looking Dracula-like face that loomed above the ground with a threateningly-evil stare and a bloody, sneeringly-fanged mouth.

LESSON 2

8. Though Figure 1 diagrammatically shows the various supersensible bodies and vehicles of expression layered on top of the physical body, the esotericist understands that the various forms of consciousness actually pervade, permeate and interpenetrate each other.

9. Rene Descartes (1596–1650) was an influential philosopher, mathematician and scientist. He is also well-known for developing the Cartesian coordinate system in mathematics.

10. The inner experience of completely silencing the soul-

activity of thinking has been accurately and poetically expressed in the Beatles' song, "Tomorrow Never Knows":

Turn off your mind, relax and float down stream;
It is not dying, it is not dying.

Lay down all thoughts, surrender to the void;
It is shining, it is shining.

Yet you may see the meaning of within;
It is being, it is being ...

11. Of course the condition of nirvana as envisioned in Buddhism is an after-death occurrence that is much more permanent. This is the reason why the mental stillness that occurs during the crucifixion experience is here entitled "a foretaste" of nirvana.

12. According to esoteric science, the astral body has a number of spinning centres of vital-energy called "chakras" (Sanskrit for "wheels") that are aligned parallel to the spinal column and head. These vortices of psychic energy (also known as "lotus flowers") function as superphysical organs of perception, consciousness and life-activity.

13. Concerning the pineal gland, in a lecture given on 01 October 1911 entitled, "The Etherization of the Blood," Rudolf Steiner similarly stated:

At the moment of waking or of going to sleep ... In the man of high morality and an outstreaming intellectuality, a peaceful expansion of glimmering light appears in the region of the pineal gland. This gland is almost surrounded by a small sea of light in the moment between waking and sleeping. Moral nobility is revealed when a calm glow surrounds the pineal gland at these moments. (Published in *The Reappearance of Christ in the Etheric*; 1983)

LESSON 4

14. The terrifying, soul-shattering experience of entering the subterranean, lower-astral region of the earth has also been indicated by Rudolf Steiner; such as in the lecture given on 19 January 1922, and published in *Old and New Methods of Initiation* (1991):

> As we step over the threshold into the spiritual world we are met with a burning, scalding fire which seeks to devour everything the world of sense perceptions has to offer. We enter, without a doubt, the world of destructive forces. This is the first sight that meets us on the other side.

15. According to spiritual science, the asuras are undeveloped archai (spirits of personality) who fell behind during a primeval stage in planetary development known esoterically as the Ancient Saturn Period. As such, they are deleterious to mankind and distort human sexuality.

16. Ahrimanic beings are esoterically understood to be undeveloped archangels (spirits of fire) who fell behind during the Ancient Sun Period of planetary earth development. Their formidable leader— Satan/Ahriman— is, however, a recalcitrant power (spirit of form).

17. According to spiritual science, there are three degrees of supersensible perception that are developed through initiatory training: Imagination, Inspiration and Intuition. Spiritual forms are perceived through Imagination; spiritual interconnections and relationships are perceived through Inspiration; and it is only through Intuition (the highest supersensory development) that spiritual beings can be directly perceived.

18. Ancient Lemuria, in esoteric history, was an antediluvian land-mass that pre-dated the Atlantean Age, upon which our human ancestors first physically appeared on earth. It

was characteristically hot, fiery, volcanic, volatile and extremely dangerous.

19. In a lecture given on 12 June 1906 entitled "Earthquakes, Volcanoes and Human Will" (and published in *An Esoteric Cosmology*; 2008) Rudolf Steiner stated the following:

> If we now abstract these [top] three layers by means of our thinking, we would then find the earth in the condition in which it was before the separation of the moon [ie: the Ancient Moon Period] ...
>
> If now again in thought one were to abstract these last three [middle] layers just described, one would arrive at the condition in which our globe was when Sun, Moon and Earth were still interwoven [ie: the Ancient Sun Period] ...

20. As well as in numerous other lectures, Rudolf Steiner briefly summarized the primordial developmental stages of the earth and solar system in a lecture given on 02 February 1910, entitled "The Entrance of the Christ-being into the Evolution of Humanity":

> The earth passed through the [Ancient] Saturn, Sun and Moon ages and then only did it become the structure it is today. On [Ancient] Saturn the germ of the physical body was laid, on the [Ancient] Sun that of the etheric body, on the [Ancient] Moon that of the astral body, and the germ of the ego was added on the [Present] earth ... (Published in *The Christ Impulse and Development of the Ego-Consciousness*; 2010)

LESSON 5

21. This esoteric information was conveyed by Rudolf Steiner in a lecture presented on 01 January 1909 entitled "Mephistopheles and Earthquakes":

Then we come to the sixth stratum, the "Fire Earth", containing as "substances" within it, forces that can bring about terrible havoc and destruction. It is actually into these forces that the primordial Fire has been banished.

In and from this stratum the realm of Ahriman operates—in a material sense. What manifests in the phenomena of outer nature, in air and water, in cloud formations, in lightning and thunder—all this is, so to speak, a last vestige on the earth's surface, of forces that were already connected with ancient Saturn and separated from the earth together with the sun. By what is working in these forces, the inner fire-forces of the earth are placed in the service of Ahriman. There he has the center of his activity; and whereas his spiritual influences make their way to the souls of men and lead them to error, we see how Ahriman—in a certain respect shackled—has certain foci for his activity in the interior of the earth. (Published in *The Deed of Christ and the Opposing Spiritual Powers*; 1976)

22. According to Revelation:

> Then I saw another beast which rose out of the earth; it had two horns like a lamb and it spoke like a dragon ... let him who has understanding reckon the number of the beast, for it is a human number, its number is six hundred and sixty-six. (Rev 13: 11,18)

LESSON 6

23. In a lecture delivered on 02 June 1906 entitled "The Astral World" Rudolf Steiner stated the following:

> How are we to conceive of the astral world? The

three different worlds of which occultism speaks are as follows:

(1) The physical world.

(2) The astral world (Purgatory).

(3) The spiritual world, or Devachan in Sanskrit terminology (The Christian Heaven).

24. Theosophical writer, Andrew Rooke, in an article written in "Sunrise" magazine (1987) well-explained the esoteric understanding of the three outermost "planets":

> In theosophy Uranus, Neptune, and Pluto differ from the sacred planets which latter are closely related with the destiny of earth. They do not strictly belong to our solar system, but have been captured by the gravitational energy of the sun. Although Uranus belongs to our "universal solar system," and is intimately linked with the destiny of the sun, Neptune, and perhaps Pluto, ventured into the outer reaches of our system, possibly during the chaos of solar and planetary formation billions of years ago (cf. *Fountain-Source*, pp. 324-5). Theosophists compare this process with the micro-universe of the atom that captures and discards electrons. Similarly, Neptune, and perhaps Pluto, will one day leave the solar system. However, as in the atomic world, Pluto, and especially Neptune, vitally affect the "magnetism" of the solar system and thus life here on earth billions of miles away.

LESSON 7

25. It is, of course, recognized here that the spiritual-scientific conception of Christ-Jesus is different and more complex than the simpler, conventional understanding of Jesus

Christ. Though some theologians and believers may unfortunately consider this alternate version to be heretical, to esoteric-Christians it is simply a deeper and more comprehensive understanding of the mysterious nature of Our Saviour that remains difficult to completely understand.

26. While the inexperienced non-initiate is probably unfamiliar with the Bodhisattva Vow; nevertheless, the voluntary decision to compassionately return to earth-existence for the sake of others aligns them with the "Supreme Council of Twelve"—the twelve, illustrious bodhisattva-beings who oversee and guide earthly-evolution under the divine leadership of Christ-Jesus.

27. In his definitive book on modern-day Rosicrucian initiation, entitled *Knowledge of the Higher Worlds and its Attainment* (1986), Rudolf Steiner described the Bodhisattva Vow in a more-detailed, spiritual-scientific way. The voice of one's Christ-infused God-self is here termed "the greater guardian of the threshold"; and the guardian's words of spiritual advice are stated as follows:

> "Thou hast released thyself from the world of the senses. Thou hast won the right to become a citizen of the supersensible world, whence thine activity can now be directed. For thine own sake, thou dost no longer require thy physical body in its present form. If thine intention were merely to acquire the faculties necessary for life in the supersensible world, thou needest no longer return to the sense-world ... Hitherto thou hast sought only thine own release, but now, having thyself become free, thou canst go forth as a liberator of thy fellows ... Thou wilt some day be able to unite with me, but I cannot be blessed so long as others remain unredeemed ..."

An indescribable splendor shines forth from the

second Guardian of the Threshold; union with him looms as a far distant ideal before the soul's vision. Yet there is also the certitude that this union will not be possible until all the powers afforded by this world are applied to the task of its liberation and redemption. By fulfilling the demands of the higher light-being the initiate will contribute to the liberation of the human race. He lays his gifts on the sacrificial altar of humanity. Should he prefer his own premature elevation into the supersensible world, the stream of human evolution will flow over and past him. After his liberation he can gain no new powers from the world of the senses; and if he places his work at the world's disposal it will entail his renouncement of any further benefit for himself.

CHAPTER 9

28. For a more thorough account of Christ-Jesus' after-death existence from the crucifixion to the resurrection, the interested reader is directed to this author's prior publication: *The Star of Higher Knowledge: The Five Guiding Mysteries of Esoteric Christianity* (2015); available from Amazon.com.

29. According to the *Catechism of the Catholic Church*:

But for us a new day has dawned: the day of Christ's Resurrection; the seventh day completes the first creation; the eighth day begins the new creation. Thus, the work of creation culminates in the greater work of redemption. The first creation finds its meaning and its summit in the new creation in Christ, the splendour of which surpasses that of the first creation. (Paragraph 349)

30. As understood by esoteric science, the true physical body is actually an invisible human form comprised of super-fine, elemental matter that shapes and molds denser physical substance into a functioning physical constitution. Referred to as the "physical phantom" in spiritual-scientific writing, this archetypal human form was destined to remain physically ephemeral and invisible.

    But instead, as a result of luciferic and ahrimanic interference in the early stages of human evolution, the physical phantom began to increasingly attract denser and denser chemical components. Over time, the densifying human form solidified to the degree of physical visibility. This resulted in the human body becoming increasingly subject to the terrestrial force of gravity and to the chemical forces of disintegration (ie: the forces of death).

    By freeing his own physical phantom from sorathic densification and rigidification, Christ-Jesus "redeemed" the human body for all mankind to duplicate; and thereby for each individual to transcend any participation in bodily death.

31. In the brief time that Christ-Jesus discarded his perfectly-preserved body and soul vehicles after death, these redeemed vehicles began to rapidly multiply themselves into numerous, exact replicas preserved in supersensible space. Remarkably, these replicated Christ-vehicles can be mystically incorporated and intrapsychically employed by worthy disciples of our Saviour. (For more information, please refer to Chapter 5 in *The Star of Higher Knowledge*; 2015, by this author)

CONCLUSION

32. In biology, it is understood that for an egg to reproduce (ie: to grow and expand) it must be fertilized. A seed is

defined as the fertilized egg of a plant.

33. Celestial beings, such as angels and archangels—since their forms are superphysical—do not of course experience physical death. Nevertheless, they still alternate between periods of activity and rest; as well as experience evolutionary periods of transformation and change.

34. Of course, single-celled organisms (such as bacteria) don't need to generate a miniature, single-celled genetic blueprint of themselves in order to reproduce—they already exist as a single cell. They simply duplicate themselves, usually by asexual reproduction.

35. The noticeable similarity between sleep and death was touched on by Rudolf Steiner in a lecture given on 10 December 1912, in which he stated:

> When the human being sleeps during his earthly existence, that is to say when he has left his physical and etheric bodies and is living in his Ego and astral body which are then in the world of stars, he too is actually in that world. And it is a fact that our condition in sleep is objectively far more similar to the condition between death and rebirth than is usually imagined. Objectively, the two conditions are very similar. The only difference is that during sleep in normal life the human being has no consciousness of the world in which he is living, whereas between death and the new birth he is conscious of what is happening to him. That is the essential difference. If the human being were to awake in his Ego and astral body when these members are outside his physical body during sleep he would be in the same condition as he is between death and the new birth. The difference is actually only a state of consciousness. (Published in *Between Death and Rebirth*; 1975)

36. Regarding the typical lack of conscious awareness during sleep, Rudolf Steiner in the same lecture quoted above, similarly stated:

> [D]uring sleep the human being has no consciousness. Why not? The reason is that he is not meant to witness what happens to him during sleep. During sleep the forces used up during waking life are restored and man is not meant to witness this process, which is the antithesis of what is in operation during waking life and is concealed from human consciousness ... We can therefore say that the whole life-giving, restorative process is concealed from man's conscious life on Earth. Processes of perception, of cognition, lie within the field of his consciousness; the life-giving process does not. (Ibid)

ADDENDUM

37. As explained by Rudolf Steiner in a lecture given on 06 June 1907, entitled "The Nature of Initiation" (and published in *Rosicrucian Wisdom: An Introduction*; 2005) :

> These are the two paths of esoteric training particularly fitted for the West. All that is connected with our culture and the life we lead and must lead is lifted up, raised into the principle of initiation through the [Mystic-]Christian and through the Rosicrucian[-Christian] training. The purely [Mystic-]Christian way is somewhat difficult for modern man, hence the Rosicrucian[-Christian] path has been introduced for those who have to live in the present age. If someone would take the old purely [Mystic-]Christian path in the midst of modern life he must be able to cut himself off for a time from the world outside, in

order to enter it again later all the more intensively.
On the other hand the Rosicrucian[-Christian] path
can be followed by all, no matter in what occupation
or sphere of life they may be placed.

SELECT BIBLIOGRAPHY

(in alphabetical order)

- *Catechism of the Catholic Church* (Our Sunday Visitor, Publishing Division, 2000)

- Holy Bible, *RSV-CE* (Ignatius Press, 2006)

- Ron MacFarlane, *The Greater Mysteries of the Divine Trinity, the Logos-Word and Creation* (Greater Mysteries Publications, 2015)

- Ron MacFarlane, *The Star of Higher Knowledge: The Five Guiding Mysteries of Esoteric Christianity* (Greater Mysteries Publications, 2015)

- Rudolf Steiner, *An Esoteric Cosmology* (Wilder Publications, 2008)

- Rudolf Steiner, *Between Death and Rebirth* (Rudolf Steiner Press, 1975)

- Rudolf Steiner, *From Jesus to Christ* (Rudolf Steiner Press, 1973)

- Rudolf Steiner, *Knowledge of the Higher Worlds and its Attainment* (The Anthroposophic Press, 1986)

- Rudolf Steiner, *Life Between Death and Rebirth* (Anthroposophic Press, 1985)

- Rudolf Steiner, *Man: Hieroglyph of the Universe* (Rudolf Steiner Press, 1972)

- Rudolf Steiner, *Man's Being, His Destiny and World-Evolution* (The Anthroposophic Press, 1966)

- Rudolf Steiner, *Old and New Methods of Initiation* (Rudolf Steiner Press, 1991)

- Rudolf Steiner, *Rosicrucian Wisdom: An Introduction* (Rudolf Steiner Press, 2005)

- Rudolf Steiner, Lecture entitled "The Astral World" (02 June 1906)

- Rudolf Steiner, *The Christ Impulse and Development of the Ego-Consciousness* (Kessinger Publishing, 2010)

- Rudolf Steiner, *The Deed of Christ and the Opposing Spiritual Powers* (Steiner Book Centre, 1976)

- Rudolf Steiner, Lecture entitled "The Interior of the Earth and Volcanic Eruptions" (16 April 1906)

- Rudolf Steiner, *The Reappearance of Christ in the Etheric* (The Anthroposophic Press, 1983)

OTHER BOOKS BY

RON MACFARLANE

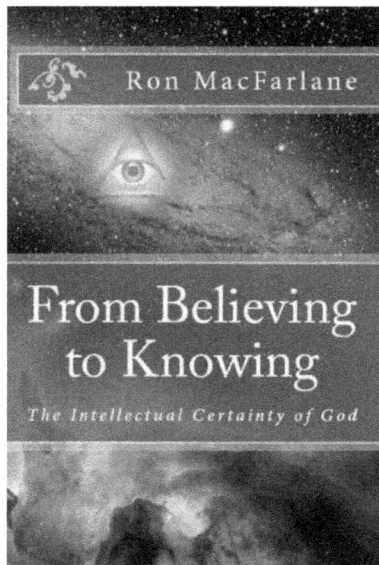

THERE IS a puzzling and pervasive misconception in present-day thinking that the existence of God cannot be intellectually determined, and that mentally accepting the existence of God is strictly a matter of non-rational belief (faith).

As such, contemplating God's existence is erroneously regarded as the exclusive subject of faith-based or speculative ideologies (religion and philosophy) which have no proper place in natural scientific study.

The fact is, there are a number of very convincing intellectual arguments concerning the existence of God that have been around for hundreds of years. Indeed, the existence of God can be determined with compelling intellectual certainty—provided the thinker honestly wishes to do so. Moreover, recent advances and discoveries in science have not weakened previous intellectual arguments for God's existence, but instead have enormously strengthened and supported them.

Intellectually assenting to the existence of God is easily demonstrated to be a superlatively logical conclusion, not some vague irrational conceptualization. Remarkably, at the present time there are only two seriously-competing intellectual explanations of life: the existence of God (the "God-hypothesis") and the existence of infinite universes (the "multiverse theory"). The postulation of an infinite number of unobservable universes is clearly a desperate attempt by atheistic scientists to avoid the God-hypothesis as the most credible and logical intellectual explanation of life and the universe. Moreover, under intellectual scrutiny, the scientifically celebrated "evolutionary theory" is here demonstrated to be fatally-flawed (philosophically illogical) as a credible explanation of life.

In this particular discourse, five well-known intellectual arguments for God's existence will be thoroughly examined. In considering these arguments, every attempt has been made to include current contributions, advances and discoveries that have modernized the more traditional arguments. Prior to examining these particular arguments for God, the universal predilection to establish intellectual 'oneness'—"monism"—will be considered in detail as well as the recurring propensity to postulate the existence of one supreme being—"monotheism."

Once intellectual certainty of one Supreme Being is established, a number of divine attributes can be logically deduced as well. Eleven of these attributes will be determined and examined in greater detail.

This book is available to order from Amazon.com

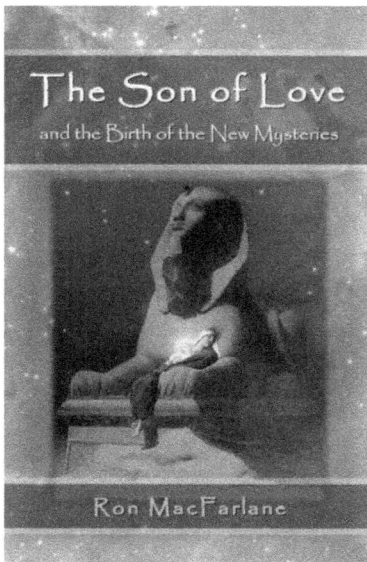

The Son of Love
and the Birth of the New Mysteries

Ron MacFarlane

FOR COUNTLESS esoteric students today, the Mystery centres of ancient times have retained a powerful and fascinating allure. Moreover, there is often a wishful longing to revive and continue their secretive initiatory activity into modern times.

Unfortunately, this anachronistic longing is largely based on an illusionary misunderstanding of these Mysteries and the real reasons for their destined demise.

The primary reason for the disappearance of the ancient Mysteries is that they have been supplanted by the superior new mysteries—the mysteries of the Son. These new mysteries were initiated by Christ-Jesus himself. In order to better understand these Son-mysteries in a spiritually-scientific way, Rudolf Steiner (1861–1925) established the Anthroposophical Movement and Society.

Unfortunately, anthroposophy today has become unduly influenced by members and leaders who long to transform spiritual science into a modern-day Mystery institution. Moreover, contrary to his own words and intentions, Rudolf Steiner is even claimed to be the founder of some new "Michael-Mysteries."

By carefully establishing a correct esoteric understanding of the ancient pagan Mysteries, as well as a better appreciation of the new mysteries of the Son, this well-researched and readable discourse convincingly shows that all current and past attempts to revive the ancient pagan Mysteries regressively diverts human development backward to the seducer of mankind, Lucifer, rather than progressively forward to the saviour of mankind, Christ-Jesus.

Moreover, by additionally tracing the intriguing historical

development of esoteric Christianity (particularly the Knights of the Holy Grail and Rosicrucianism) alongside Freemasonry, the Knights Templar and Theosophy, this important and necessary study illuminates the correct esoteric position and true significance of anthroposophical spiritual science.

This book is available to order from Amazon.com

Physical Science to Spiritual Science

The Future Development of Intellectual Thought

Ron MacFarlane

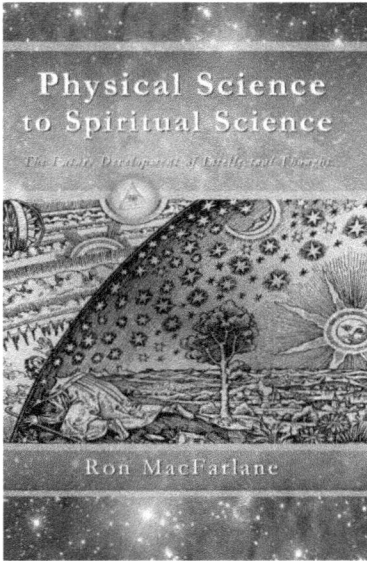

THE PRIDE OF civilized mankind—intellectual thinking—is at a critical crossroads today. No doubt surprising to many, the cognitive capacity to consciously formulate abstract ideas in the mind, and then to manipulate them according to devised rules of logic in order to acquire new knowledge has only been humanly possible for about the last 3,000 years. Prior to intellectual (abstract) thinking, mental activity characteristically consisted of vivid pictorial images that arose spontaneously in the human mind from natural and supernatural stimuli.

The ability to think abstractly is the necessary foundation for mathematics, language and empirical science. The developmental history of intellectual thought, then, exactly parallels the developmental history of mathematics, language and science. Moreover, since abstract thinking inherently encourages the cognitive separation of subject (the thinker) and object (the perceived environment), the history of intellectual development also parallels the historical development of self-conscious (ego) awareness.

Over the last 3000 years, mankind in general has slowly perfected intellectual thinking; and thereby developed complex mathematics, sophisticated languages, comprehensively-detailed empirical sciences and pronounced ego-awareness. Unfortunately, all this intellectual activity over the many previous centuries has also exclusively strengthened human awareness of the physical, material world and substantially decreased awareness of the superphysical spiritual world.

That is why today, intellectual thinking is at a critical crossroads in further development. Thinking (intellectual or otherwise) is a superphysical activity—an activity within the soul. Empirical science is incorrect in postulating that physical brain tissue generates thought. The brain is simply the biological "sending and receiving" apparatus: sending sense-perceptions to the soul and receiving thought-conceptions from the soul. All this activity certainly generates chemical and electrical activity within the brain; but this activity is the effect, not the cause of thinking.

The danger to future intellectual thought is that increased acceptance of the erroneous scientific notion that thinking is simply brain-chemistry will increasingly deny and deaden true superphysical thinking. Future thinking runs the risk of becoming "a self-fulfilled prophecy"—the more people fervently believe that thought is simply brain-chemistry, the more thought will indeed become simply brain-chemistry. As a result, future human beings will be less responsible for generating their own thinking activity and more involuntarily controlled by their own brain chemistry. The artificial intelligence of machines won't become more human; but instead human beings will become more like robotic machines.

Presently, then, empirical science is leading intellectual thinking in a downward, materialistic direction. Correspondingly, however, true spiritual science (anthroposophy) is also actively engaged in leading intellectual thought back to its superphysical source in the soul. *Physical Science to Spiritual Science: the Future Development of Intellectual Thought* begins by examining the historical development of intellectual thinking and the corresponding rise of physical science. Once this has been discussed, practical and detailed information is presented on how spiritual science is leading intellectual thinking back to its true soul-source. It is intended that upon completion of this discourse, sincere and open-minded readers will themselves come to experience the exhilarating, superphysical nature of their own intellectual thought.

This book is available to order from Amazon.com

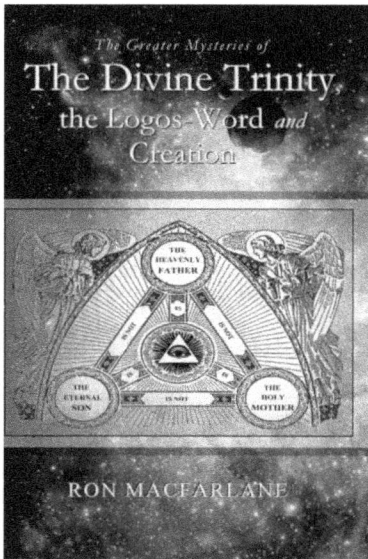

THE DIVINE TRINITY—the greatest of all Christian mysteries. How is it that the one God is a unity of three divine persons? Christ-Jesus first revealed this mystery to his disciples when on earth. Later, around the sixth century, the Trinitarian mystery was theologically clarified and outlined by the formulation of the Athanasian Creed. Conceptual understanding of the divine Trinity has changed very little in Western society since then. Similarly with the theological understanding of the Logos-Word, as mentioned in the Gospel of St. John. The traditional understanding, that has remained essentially unchallenged for centuries, is that the Logos-Word is synonymous with God the Son. As for creation, the best that mainstream Christianity has historically provided is an ancient, allegorical account contained in the Book of Genesis.

Out of the hidden well-springs of esoteric Christianity, and as the title indicates, *The Greater Mysteries of the Divine Trinity, the Logos-Word and Creation*, delves much more deeply into the profound mysteries of the Trinitarian God, the Logos-Word of St. John and the creation of the universe. The divine Trinity is here demonstrated to be the loving union of Heavenly Father, Holy Mother and Eternal Son. The Logos-Word is here evidenced to be the "Universal Man," the primordial cosmic creation of God the Son. Universal creation itself is here detailed to be the "one life becoming many"—the multiplication of the Logos-Word into countless individualized life-forms and beings.

The depth and breadth of original and thought-provoking information presented here will, no doubt, stimulate and excite those esoteric thinkers who are seriously seeking answers to the deeper mysteries of life, existence and the universe.

This book is available to order from Amazon.com

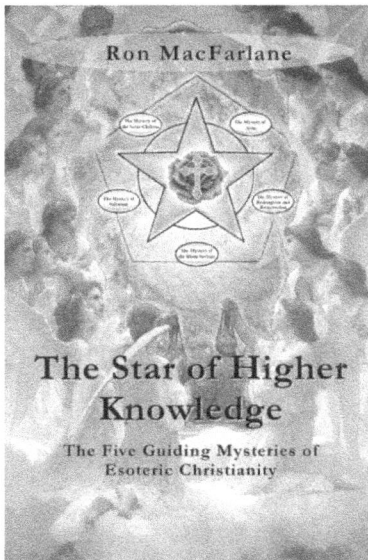

WHEN CHRIST-JESUS walked the earth over two thousand years ago, he established a two-fold division in his teaching that has continued to this day. To the general public, he simplified his teaching and presented it in pictorial, allegorical and figurative imagery in the form of stories, parables and lessons that could be imaginatively and intuitively understood.

To his inner circle of disciples (who were sufficiently prepared), however, he taught intellectual concepts, clear ideas and logical reasoning that could be understood on a much deeper and wider level of comprehension. As biblically explained:

> Then the disciples came and said to him, "Why do you speak to them [the general public] in parables?" And he answered them, "To you it has been given to know the secrets of the kingdom of heaven, but to them it has not been given ... This is why I speak to them in parables, because seeing they do not see, and hearing they do not hear, nor do they understand." (Matt 13:10, 13)

Moreover, in union with the divine, Our Saviour was able to reveal sacred knowledge that had never been previously presented in the entire history of mankind: "I will explain mysteries hidden since the creation of the world" (Matt 13:35). This sacred and revealed knowledge has been termed "Christ-mysteries" or "mysteries of the Son."

After his glorious resurrection and ascension, Christ-Jesus

institutionalized his two-fold mystery-teachings through St. Peter and St. John (the evangelist, not the apostle). Through St. Peter, Our Saviour instituted a universal Christian *religion* and *theology* to preserve, promote and convey the more basic and simplified mystery-teachings that are intended for the general public. Through St. John, Christ-Jesus instituted a universal Christian *philosophy* and *theosophy* to preserve, promote and convey the more comprehensive and complex mystery-teachings that are intended for the more advanced disciples (Christian initiates). In esoteric terminology, the institutionalized teachings through St. Peter are known as the "lesser mysteries of exoteric Christianity." The institutionalized teachings through St. John are known as the "greater mysteries of esoteric Christianity."

While both mystery-teaching approaches are equally sacred, profound and intended to complement each other, corrupt and intolerant authorities within the universal institution (Church) of St. Peter, for many centuries, persecuted and attacked any public expressions of esoteric Christianity. Consequently, genuine historical forms of esoteric Christianity, such as the Knights of the Holy Grail and the Fraternity of the Rose-Cross, were forced to be secretive and publically-hidden during the past two thousand years.

Thankfully today, the social, political and intellectual climate has progressed to the point where the greater mystery-teachings of esoteric Christianity can begin to be publically revealed for the first time. This modern-day outpouring really began with the twentieth-century establishment of anthroposophy by Rudolf Steiner (1861–1925). The information and approach presented in *The Star of Higher Knowledge: The Five Guiding Mysteries of Esoteric Christianity* is intended to augment and continue the mystery-teachings of Christ-Jesus as safeguarded by the Rosicrucian Fraternity and publicized through anthroposophy.

Consequently, this particular discourse delves much more deeply and comprehensively into the cosmos-changing salvational achievement of Christ-Jesus: the historical and cosmic preparations; as well as his birth, life, death, resurrection and ascension. While much of this mystery information may be unfamiliar, unknown and unexpected to mainstream (exoteric) Christianity, it in no way is meant to criticize, denigrate or displace the profound teachings of the universal Church; but rather, to complement, to enhance and to enlarge—for the betterment of true Christianity and, thereby, the betterment of all mankind.

This book is available to order from Amazon.com

Also check out the authour's website:

www.heartofshambhala.com

A Site Dedicated to True Esoteric Christianity

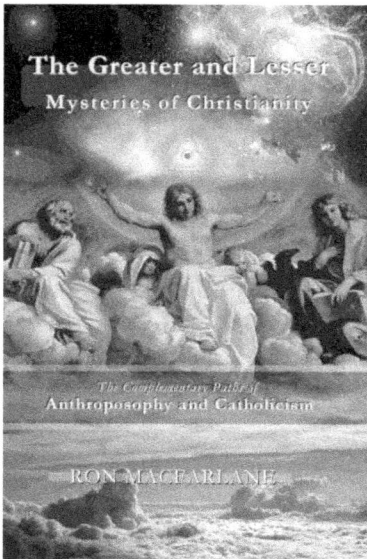

Contemporary Christianity, the world religion established by the God-Man, Christ-Jesus, and founded on the revelatory-principle that "God is love," is hardly the shining example of ideological unity and universal brotherhood that it was intended to be. There are approximately 41,000 different Christian denominations in the world today, many of which are fervently hostile to each other.

Atheistic and anti-Christian polemicists have concluded that there is something inherently wrong with Christianity itself and, in consequence, it is doomed to failure and eventual extinction.

Discerning Christian advocates, however, know that any apparent failure to realize the high ideals of Christianity is not due to the profound teachings and the illustrious life-example of Christ-Jesus, but instead to the limitations of wounded human nature. Corrupt, power-hungry, destructive and evil-minded human beings have twisted, distorted and fragmented true Christianity for the past two thousand years, and continue to do so today.

Moreover, on a much deeper spiritual level, since Christianity is indeed a divinely-initiated endeavor to help restore "fallen" humanity, powerful and demonic beings have attempted to destroy nascent Christianity from its very inception. But thankfully, according to Christ-Jesus himself, "the powers of hell will not prevail against it [Christianity]" (Matt 16:18).

Sadly contributing to the injurious fragmentation of Christianity—the "religion of divine love"—is the sectarian hostility between certain proponents of anthroposophy and select members of the Catholic Church. In both cases, this is largely due to ignorance; that is, an almost complete lack of understanding about the true significance and mission of the other—anthroposophical critics know almost nothing of Catholicism, and Catholic critics know almost nothing about anthroposophy.

The wonderful reconciliatory fact is that anthroposophy and Catholicism are not conflicting polar opposites, but are instead like two sides of the same golden coin—different, but complementary. Instead of only one side or the other being the only true approach to Christ-Jesus, both are uniquely necessary and both positively contribute to the complete truth of Christianity.

Since this author is happily and harmoniously both an anthroposophist and a Catholic, *The Greater and Lesser Mysteries of Christianity: The Complementary Paths of Anthroposophy and Catholicism* earnestly seeks to correct the misinformation and lack of understanding that each partisan critic has for the other. As in almost every significant dispute, increased knowledge and familiarity about each other will in time bring both sides closer together for mutual growth and benefit.

This book is available to order from Amazon.com

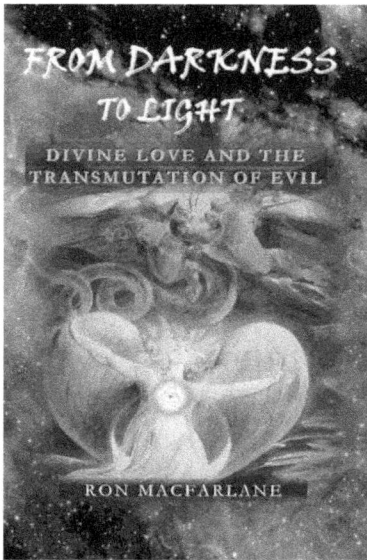

FROM DARKNESS TO LIGHT

DIVINE LOVE AND THE TRANSMUTATION OF EVIL

RON MACFARLANE

IN THE LIGHT of spiritual science, never before in the history of the world has there been such an assailment of supernatural evil upon humanity as extensive and intense as there exists at the present time. Subconsciously pouring into the human soul are the seductive whisperings of Luciferic beings and fallen angels; the perceptual distortions of Ahrimanic (Satanic) beings; the lurid, egocentric promptings of corrupt spirits of personality (asuras); and the violent inducements of blood-lust rising up from the subterranean "beast of Revelation" (Sorath the sun-demon).

The tragic and bitter irony of all this, however, is that because of today's pervasive, atheistic and secular culture and the materialistic worldview of natural science, individual human beings are correspondingly the most oblivious to supernatural evil than they have ever been at any other time in world history.

To be sure, people today are certainly aware of the *effects* of supernatural evil—extensive and increased natural disasters; horrific instances of mass genocide; the prolific use of torture and brutality by government agencies; individual acts of sudden cruelty and murder; pathological selfishness throughout the world's business and financial markets; strange, globally-infectious viral contagions; the devaluation of human life through abortion and euthanasia; and a world-wide pandemic of dehumanizing drug addiction. What most people today fail to realize is that the invisible fomenting agents—the *causes*—of all these life-threatening, destructive physical events and pathologies are ultimately rooted in the impulses of supernatural evil.

To be sure, mankind would have completely and totally succumbed to this tsunami of supernatural evil if it weren't for the protective and opposing intervention of powerful, benevolent celestial beings, such as St. Michael the Archai, Yahweh-Elohim (the spirit of the moon), and the Solar-Christos (aka: "Christ"—the regent of the sun).

More than ever, it is crucially important in today's world to understand the nature of evil, and to become more aware and cognizant of the various perpetrators of supernatural evil. Thereby, conscious cooperation with the compassionate protectors and guardians of mankind can be increased and strengthened, so that supernatural evil is better resisted and eventually overcome.

To this end, *From Darkness to Light: Divine Love and the Transmutation of Evil* delves deeply into the thorny questions of "What exactly is evil?"; together with "How and when did evil begin?"; as well as "Why does God allow evil to exist?" Once the nature, genesis and purpose of evil is better understood, then various influential superphysical perpetrators of supernatural evil will be examined in closer detail. Correspondingly, the superphysical proponents of cosmic holiness will be identified and better understood as well.

Wherever possible, the spiritual-scientific research of anthroposophy—an independent offshoot of the Rosicrucian Fraternity, and the modern-day expression of esoteric Christianity that was established by Rudolf Steiner (1861–1925)—will be included and referenced. Following this profoundly-esoteric background, the destined human struggle with continuing and obdurate evil—far into the future development of the earth—will also be mentally envisioned and supersensibly examined.

It is sincerely intended that upon completion of the entire written discourse, concerned individuals will be better armed and shielded in order to become actively engaged on the side of holiness and spiritual light in the prolonged cosmic battle against evil and material darkness.

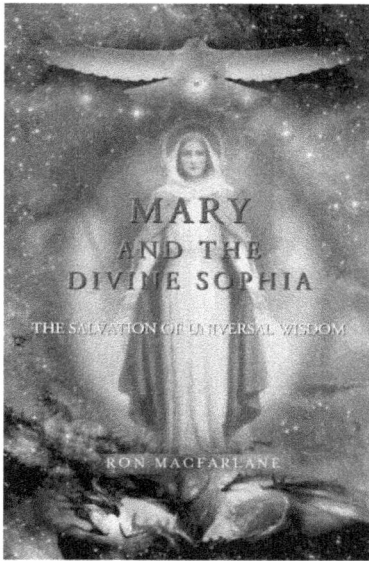

NO DOUBT, anyone interested in Christian esotericism will have noticed that there is a widespread modern-day revival of interest in the ancient gnostic concept of "Sophia" amongst a strange diversity of groups: wiccans, neo-pagans, New Agers, neo-gnostics, Catholic mystics, Orthodox Christians, radical feminists and anthropos-ophists. Adding to this ideological mélange is the exotic variety of Sophia designations and conceptions: the Divine Sophia, the heavenly-sophia, the earthly-sophia, Hagia Sophia, the goddess Sophia, the Aeon Sophia, the Virgin Sophia, Sophia-Achamoth, Pistis Sophia, Isis-Sophia, Jesus Sophia, theo-sophia, philo-sophia and anthropo-sophia.

Not surprisingly, then, this cacophony of Sophias is very often contradictory, confusing, distorted, invented, erroneous, and (sadly) rarely enlightening. It is not difficult to detect that "esoteric entrepreneurs" have seized this current "thirst for Sophia" to offer up a potpourri of books, courses, conferences, workshops, lessons, websites, video clips, internet articles—even worship services—to inundate, titillate and financially captivate any novice Sophia seeker.

So, what is a sincere Christian esotericist to make of this fervent Sophia phenomenon: "Is it a positive and healthy spiritual development, or is it a regressive and outmoded religious diversion?" This particular discourse—*Mary and the Divine Sophia*—delves deeply and genuinely into this important question in order to establish spiritual fact from unspiritual fiction.

In order to adequately answer this question, however, profound esoteric investigation into the Trinitarian nature of God, as well as the universal being of the Logos-Word, together with the fundamental underlying principles of the created cosmos will need to be detailed and discussed. Some of this previously-guarded esoteric information may be quite new and unfamiliar to many readers; but every effort has been made to present it in clear, understandable concepts.

Furthermore, since the mother of Jesus is very often intimately associated or connected to historical and present-day conceptions of Sophia, a comprehensive study will also be undertaken regarding Mary and her special relationship to the Divine Sophia; relying heavily on the spiritual-scientific research of Austrian philosopher and esotericist, Rudolf Steiner (1861–1925). Once again, a great deal of this information will be startlingly new to those unfamiliar with anthroposophy; but, as before, great care has been taken to present this possibly-unfamiliar information in a comprehensible, intellectually-accessible way.

It is sincerely intended that this discourse will provide the earnest esotericist with reliable, trustworthy and objective spiritual knowledge in order to confidently know and understand the mystery-truth of the heavenly-sophia; and thereby extricate her from the distortions and falsifications of Lucifer and Ahriman.

This book is available to order from Amazon.com

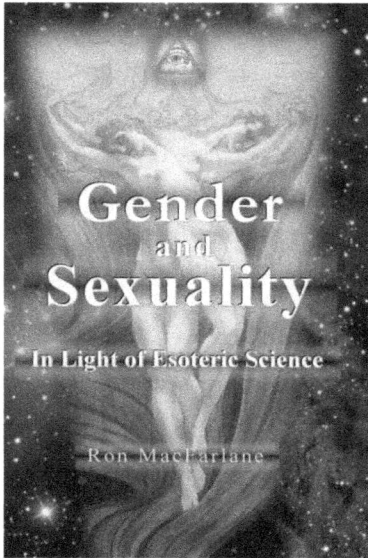

Gender
and
Sexuality

In Light of Esoteric Science

Ron MacFarlane

SINCE THE DAWN of mankind, human beings have unquestioningly accepted the self-evident biological truth that there are only two distinct sexes—male and female. Furthermore, this truth was understood to be divinely established, as indicated in the ancient Hebrew writings of Moses: "So God created man in his own image ... male and female he created them. And God blessed them" (Gen 1:27, 28).

Similarly with the concomitant truth that there are only two distinct genders—masculine and feminine. Moreover, in ancient times the dual genders were seen as fundamental and complementary universal principles that infused and fashioned everything in the created cosmos. One familiar expression of this ancient metaphysical belief is the Chinese Taoist principles of yin and yang.

Throughout history, stable and productive family units, tribal groupings, social communities, and even vast empires were globally established on the exigent foundational truths of sexuality and gender—that is—until very recently.

Beginning in the mid-1950s, what had been perennially and universally accepted regarding sex and gender began to be academically questioned and challenged. This ideological heterodoxy quickly accelerated in the 1960s with the inception and radical cultural impact of the sexual revolution and the feminist movement. Increased and well-organized gay and lesbian activism in the 1970s also did much to publicly reject the traditional dichotomies of male–female and masculine–feminine in order to promote a novel range of non-normative sexualities and exotic gender categories.

By the early 2000s, sociological theorists, academic institutions, media organizations, civil rights groups, medical associations, political parties, national governments and international agencies were all becoming involved in a cultural drive to "mainstream" this radically-new and socially-transformative gender ideology.

But to a large percentage of today's citizens throughout Western society, this cultural revolution of gender ideology has been unexpectedly and uninvitedly infiltrating their established lives and communities with a discordant cacophony of bizarre sexual and gender ideas, terms and expressions; such as: gender identity, gender expression, gender roles, gender socialization, gender fluidity, gender ambiguity (ambigender), third gender (trigender), non-binary gender, non-gender, gender neutral, agender, gender dysphoria, gender perspective, genderqueer, biological gender, hormonal gender, gonadic gender, cisgender, pangender, transgender, sexual orientation, bisexual, transsexual, intersexual, omnisexual, asexual, androgynous and two-spirit.

While even to casual observation, it is evident that this contemporary sexual revolution is causing fierce political and social upheaval, what can be perplexing to a deeper spiritual analysis are questions such as: "What exactly are sexuality and gender; and are they synonymous or different? What is causing the current sexual revolution? Why is it occurring at this particular time in world history? Is this sexual revolution progressive or regressive; beneficial or harmful? Are there spiritual forces and beings involved in this upheaval; and are they godly or evil?"

Though these questions can certainly be spiritually addressed by traditional Western theology, a much deeper, meaningful, lasting and comprehensive understanding can only be provided by the superphysical research and hidden wisdom of esoteric science.

This particular discourse, then—*Gender and Sexuality in Light of Esoteric Science*—heavily relies on ancient Yogic teachings, age-old Egyptian Hermetic philosophy, hidden Rosicrucian wisdom and the anthroposophical research of clairvoyant investigator, Rudolf Steiner (1861–1925) to profoundly and penetratingly address these important questions.

Esoteric science will convincingly explain why there are, in reality, only two sexes—male and female; and only two genders—masculine and feminine. Anything else is an unreal and delusional abstraction, hypothesis or conjecture.

In order to rationally embrace the binary truth of gender—masculine and feminine—it will be necessary to first understand the Trinitarian nature of God, and then perceive how the divine nature is faithfully reflected throughout the created universe, including human existence. After which, in order to similarly embrace the binary truth of human sexuality—male and female—it will be necessary to clairvoyantly trace the history and development of mankind on earth, back to far-distant primordial ages.

It will be shown that throughout human existence on earth, powerful supernatural beings and forces—both beneficial and inimical—have been intimately and significantly involved in the evolution and development of human sexuality. Moreover, despite the appalling lack of contemporary human awareness, this supernatural involvement has continued into the present day.

The much-celebrated "freedoms" brought about by the sexual revolution will be seen and understood to be an inimical supernatural assault on reason, reality, nature and progressive human evolution, particularly by Luciferic and Ahrimanic beings and forces.[2] The current state of sexual and gender confusion, therefore, is not regarded as a positive development by esoteric science; but rather a seriously-harmful and seductive delusionary entrapment that must be challenged, arrested and positively corrected.

This book is available to order from Amazon.com

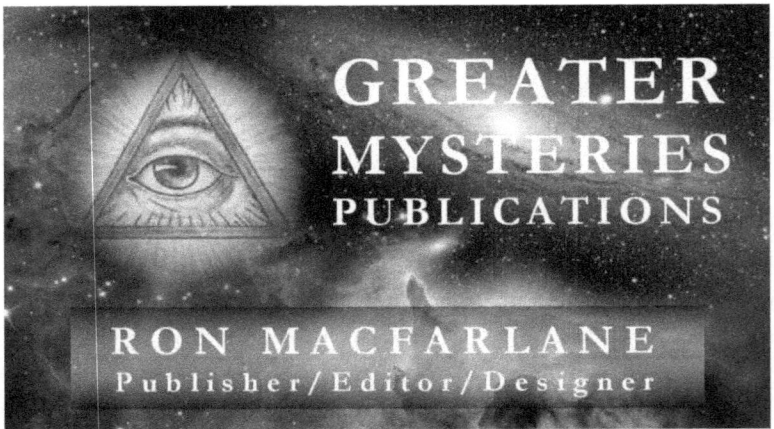

GREATER
MYSTERIES
PUBLICATIONS

RON MACFARLANE
Publisher/Editor/Designer

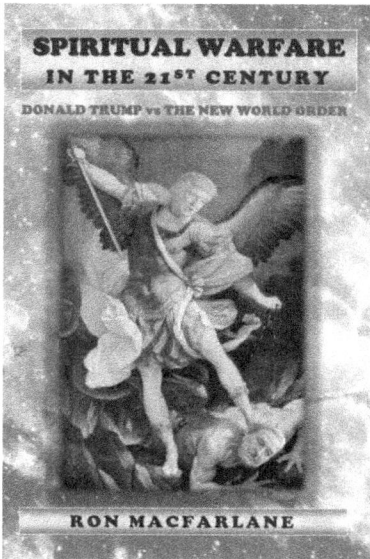

SPIRITUAL WARFARE
IN THE 21ST CENTURY
DONALD TRUMP vs THE NEW WORLD ORDER

RON MACFARLANE

A RATHER STRANGE and disturbing social upheaval has been covertly and pervasively occurring throughout the Western world—particularly in America—since the early 1990s. A creeping form of radical-socialism has been gradually infecting Western political parties, academic institutions, medical professions, mainstream news agencies, television and film industries, literary publishing and everyday social interaction for the past three decades.

Perplexingly ironic, as the former Soviet Union and Eastern Bloc States were finally divesting themselves of the failed and oppressive socialist/communist ideology of the past, intellectuals and ideologues throughout the Western world began to eagerly embrace and apply the fundamental tenets of radical-socialism.

This "Westernized" form of socialist ideology is unabashedly atheistic and openly hostile to religion, particularly Christianity, in all its denominational forms. Hypocritically, however, this same "atheistic-socialism" openly supports and defends Muslim believers, who are considered members of a "victimized minority."

The philosophical underpinning of atheistic-socialism is the classic Marxist belief that the social interaction of humanity throughout the ages has entirely and exclusively been a perpetual class struggle between the have-nots and the haves; the poor and the wealthy; the oppressed and the oppressors; the victims and the victimizers. In more Marxist terminology, historical class conflict has been between the "proletariat"—the peasants, labourers and workers; and the "bourgeoisie"—the nobility, landowners, and capitalists.

However, in recent times various activist groups—each one claiming "victimized" status—have adapted basic Marxist ideology to suit their own particular causes and agendas. For example, radical-feminists contend that it is men who are the real historic victimizers and that women are their primary victims. Alternatively, Black, Hispanic and Indigenous activists each claim that they are the continued victims of White, European-based culture. Homosexual activists assert that they are the victims of heterosexual, Judeo-Christian society. All these activists, therefore, blame a common oppressor for their perceived victimized condition—wealthy, White, conservative Christian men.

Moreover, in keeping with classic Marxist ideology, each of these socialist-inspired activist groups fervently believes that the solution to their perceived oppression is not gradual social change and reform; but the revolutionary overthrow of prosperous, White, Christian, male-influenced culture and society.

In essence, then, what is currently taking place throughout Western society is a fierce cultural war being waged by numerous left-leaning activist groups whose primary goal is the destruction of European-based Christian culture. In addition, their ultimate goal is to replace democratic governance through majority rule with an exclusively-atheistic, secular society where political, economic and cultural power is autocratically determined and enforced by centralized State-control that is driven by uncompromising, totalitarian-style minority activism.

In Western nations, this radical atheistic-socialism—recently termed the "alt-left"—has been opportunistically embraced by "left-wing" and "neo-liberal" political parties; but rejected by "right-wing" and "neo-conservative" political parties. Consequently, in America it is the Democratic Party (in general) that espouses and promotes alt-leftist atheistic-socialism; while the Republican Party (in general) rejects and opposes this ideology.

The radical alt-left agenda was enormously accelerated in America during the eight years (2009 to 2017) of Democratic Party

President, Barack Hussein Obama. Primarily through executive order and veto power, Obama enacted and enforced radical-socialist national and international policy on climate change, economic regulation, religion, abortion, de-militarization, same-sex marriage, gun control, immigration, taxation, free-trade and deficit spending.

Moreover, through presidential appointment, Obama politicized and "weaponized" the US intelligence community (FBI, CIA and NSA), the Justice department, the IRS, the Supreme Court and district court systems with radical-socialists and alt-left loyalists. Radical-socialist ideologues within the Democratic Party and their wealthy financial backers (such as George Soros) were totally confident that these "deep-state" operatives in government—together with the predominantly left-leaning communications media in radio, television and newspapers—would guarantee another presidential election victory in 2017.

Moreover, Soros and his billionaire cohorts in the Democratic Alliance had decided that Hillary Rodham Clinton would be the next American president; and had set up a "dirty-tricks" Democratic Party campaign organization (headed by Soros-lackey John Podesta) to further continue and advance their accelerating alt-left cultural revolution.

Despite pre-election propaganda by major leftist-media (such as ABC, CNN, MSNBC, the NY Times and Washington Post) that Hillary Clinton would win the presidential election by a "landslide victory"; despite the DNC (Democratic National Committee) and the Clinton election organizers conducting a corrupt, "shady-tactics" campaign in order to guarantee victory; and despite the Clinton campaign spending a record-breaking $1.2 billion to securely win the presidency—political newcomer and New York businessman, Donald J. Trump, derailed the entire alt-left revolutionary momentum by explosively winning the 2016 presidential election.

In the hours, days, weeks and months after Donald Trump's huge presidential victory (304 Electoral College votes to Clinton's

228), the alt-left—worldwide—went into complete emotional meltdown which quickly developed into a collective psychological malaise characterized by acute fear, paranoia, anxiety, depression, anger and hatred: labeled by conservative observers as "TDS—Trump Derangement Syndrome."

From Trump's powerful campaign speeches delineating his vision to "Make America Great Again (MAGA)," alt-leftist leaders and those supporting atheistic-socialism soon realized that their secular revolution was now in serious jeopardy. In the White House was everything they professed to hate—a wealthy, conservative, White, Christian male!

Moreover, Trump's vision for America was entirely contrary to atheistic-socialism: (1) instead of global homogeneity, this new president favours strong national sovereignty, legal immigration, enforced border control and a strong military; (2) instead of an entirely secularist society, this new president is intent on defending religious freedom and Judeo-Christian values and culture (such as pro-life, pro-marriage and pro-family); (3) instead of continuing to centralize authoritarian State control in Washington D.C., this new president has promised the American voter to "drain the swamp" of federal government corruption, to wrest economic power from the corporate and media elites, and to wrest political control from the self-serving Democratic and Republican establishments—thereby returning democratic power back to the American people.

Not surprisingly, then, the alt-left and their pervasive zealots in government, business, media communications, academia, psychiatry, intelligence agencies and movie industries have collectively declared war on Donald J. Trump. While radical-socialism publicly professes to promote tolerance, inclusion, diversity, political-correctness, minority rights and respect for others, the alt-left revolutionaries are hypocritically intent on destroying President Trump by whatever means available: Soros-funded riots, fake news reports, FBI surveillance, kangaroo-court challenges, drummed-up impeachment—even public outcries of assassination!

Since atheistic-socialism ideologically rejects divine moral-inspiration, divine good-counsel and divine wise-direction, it instead zealously strives to replace the ultimate moral authority of the one true God with the authoritarian and despotic control of a centralized State bureaucracy. In consequence, alt-left activist groups and political parties (either knowingly or unknowingly) play into the hands of unscrupulous billionaire globalists, such as George Soros, whose corrupt political agenda is to weaken America in order to covertly establish an elitist-controlled, one-world government—historically termed the "New World Order."

President Trump, then, as the peoples' representative of "middle America" (not the leftist corporate, intellectual and media elites in New York, Washington and California) has deliberately, knowingly and sacrificially taken on the stupendous task of resisting, opposing, undoing and defeating the domestic and international forces of the New World Order.

Moreover, on an even deeper and more universal level, since the atheistic alt-left has declared war on Christian persons, groups, beliefs, history, institutions and traditional values it is not just a cultural war that has been sweeping somnolent Western society during recent times; it is obviously a fierce spiritual battle as well. As such, the alt-left revolutionary "movement" unconsciously plays into the diabolical hands of dark spiritual beings, particularly the Antichrist, who are also intent on destroying Christianity and establishing their own evil world-domination and global-control in the near future.

Donald Trump, then, as the presidential defender of religious freedom and Judeo-Christian culture (in America and abroad) at this critical time in world history is clearly a "warrior of light," pre-destined by advanced spiritual forces to help bring America (and by extension, the rest of the world) back to the one true God of love. And while Donald Trump, as American president, clearly occupies a central role in this spiritual struggle, true victory over time will only be achieved when the vast majority of decent, honest, ethical, caring, religious, truthful and peace-loving citizens around the world rise up in unison to actively resist atheistic-socialism and the evil architects of the New World Order.

This book is available to order from Amazon.com